dealing with divorce

Leela Kirloskar is presently senior commissioning editor for Response, the business books imprint of SAGE Publications India Pvt Ltd. She qualified as a lawyer in 1993 and practiced law for about five years, before moving on to a less cerebral activity – creating desserts from home on order through Leela's Kitchen – for a few years. Leela switched to publishing in 2001 and worked part-time as a freelance copy editor, doing assignments for leading publishing houses and institutions in the areas of social science, business management, law, disaster management and the environment, among others. She is the author of four retold classic stories for children and co-author of a series of four original stories for early learners. Leela is a single, proud mother of two beautiful boys, Kartik (17) and Raghav (14). She enjoys baking, reading, travelling and spending time with her children.

OTHER LOTUS TITLES

Aitzaz Ahsan	*The Indus Saga: The Making of Pakistan*
Amir Mir	*The True Face of Jehadis: Inside Pakistan's Terror Networks*
Bhawana Somaaya	*Hema Malini: The Authorized Biography*
Duff Hart-Davis	*Honorary Tiger: The Life of Billy Arjan Singh*
M.J. Akbar	*India: The Siege Within*
M.J. Akbar	*Kashmir: Behind the Vale*
M.J. Akbar	*Nehru: The Making of India*
M.J. Akbar	*Riot after Riot*
M.J. Akbar	*The Shade of Swords*
M.J. Akbar	*Byline*
M.J. Akbar	*Blood Brothers: A Family Saga*
Maj. Gen. Ian Cardozo	*The Sinking of INS Khukri: What Happened in 1971*
Meghnad Desai	*Nehru's Hero Dilip Kumar: In the Life of India*
Nayantara Sahgal (ed.)	*Before Freedom: Nehru's Letters to His Sister*
Rohan Gunaratna	*Inside Al Qaeda*
Mushirul Hasan	*India Partitioned. 2 Vols*
Mushirul Hasan	*John Company to the Republic*
Mushirul Hasan	*Knowledge, Power and Politics*
Shrabani Basu	*Spy Princess: The Life of Noor Inayat Khan*
Thomas Weber	*Gandhi, Gandhism and the Gandhians*
Verghese Kurien as told to Gouri Salvi	*I Too Had a Dream*
Vir Sanghvi	*Men of Steel: Indian Business Leaders in Candid Conversation*

FORTHCOMING MADE EASY TITLES

B.K. Trehan & Madhu Trehan	*Retirement Made Easy*
Ramya Nageswaran & Smita Barooah Sanyal	*Pregnancy Facts Made Easy*

dealing with divorce made easy

The Essential Handbook

Leela Kirloskar

LOTUS COLLECTION
ROLI BOOKS

Lotus Collection

First published in 2007
The Lotus Collection
An imprint of
Roli Books Pvt. Ltd.
M-75, G.K. II Market, New Delhi 110 048
Phones: ++91 (011) 2921 2271, 2921 2782
2921 0886, Fax: ++91 (011) 2921 7185
E-mail: roli@vsnl.com; Website: rolibooks.com
Also at
Varanasi, Bangalore, Kolkata, Jaipur & Mumbai

Cover design and layout: Narendra Shahi

ISBN: 978-81-7436-511-8
Rs. 195

Typeset in Janson SSi by Roli Books Pvt. Ltd.
Printed at Rakmo Press, Okhla, New Delhi-110020

Contents

Introduction

Be not afraid of life.
Believe that life is worth living, and your belief will help create the fact.

– William James

Divorce is not an easy process to go through for any individual, emotionally or practically. It is a painful, life-changing experience during which you will find your every belief challenged. While there are plenty of books and web sites to help you deal with the emotional ups and downs, you will find only legal tomes fit for a trained lawyer to understand on the more practical and material aspects of divorce in India. There is also very little practical information about how to actually go about obtaining a divorce and what you can expect during this process. It is either too limited, or too wrapped up in legalese to be of any real use.

So, most people often do not even know the next logical step to take, apart from physical separation. The confusion about the legal procedure may also be compounded because of the conflicting emotions a person goes through after ending a bad marriage, and the overwhelming practical issues suddenly dumped on them. Added to this is the baggage of social stigma, which still exists to some degree and the withdrawal from society, which is partly protective and partly forced. With too much to cope with, the legal aspects do not dawn until months, or even a few years, later. And then you find yourself in a quagmire floundering through complicated procedures and completely dependent upon your lawyer/s to guide you through to final freedom, barely understanding what your rights are, much less your obligations.

This book attempts to explain the process of divorce in India and the legal provisions as simply as possible. India has the most complex family laws in the world. Along with the social, familial and emotional pressures you will inevitably face, it is a complicated recipe most people would not like to taste. The need for information on how to get out of bad marriages, legally, becomes of paramount importance, once the decision to divorce is finally taken. Statistics reveal a steep rise in marriages in India ending in divorce courts; in fact, 70 per cent of these figures represent young people in the age group of 25-35. Amicable separation within the first year of marriage has increased by 30 per cent since 2000, while 85 per cent went in for a divorce within the first five years of marriage.[1]

According to the last census of 2001, divorce rates have gone up sharply over recent years mainly in cities, from 4 per cent in the 1980s to 14 per cent in 2001. In Mumbai alone, the percentage shot up by 56 per cent between 1991 and 2001; according to Indian Statistical Institute figures, over 8,000 divorce petitions were filed in 2001[2] and these figures in recent years have definitely gone up. Interestingly, women make up a huge percentage of the population calling it quits in a marriage, due to mental or physical cruelty, or for other equally compelling reasons, cutting across economic and social strata, in rural and urban India. This is probably due to better education, more awareness and a greater degree of economic independence.

Due to its diversity, India has several laws under which marriages are solemnized and a divorce can be obtained. These include The Hindu Marriage Act, 1955; The Divorce Act, 1869; The Parsi Marriage and Divorce Act, 1936; The Dissolution of Muslim Marriage Act, 1939; The Muslim Women (Protection of Rights on Divorce) Act, 1986; The Special Marriage Act, 1956; and The Foreign Marriage Act, 1969. The basic provisions of these acts regarding how to obtain a divorce have been explained as clearly and concisely as possible. Discussions with professionals also provide the reader with a practical viewpoint of the entire procedure.

Over the years, several amendments to these acts and a few

new ones, such as the recent, much lauded The Protection of Women from Domestic Violence Act, 2005, have ensured the slow but steady progress and recognition of individual rights. While there is certainly scope for much more for fair and progressive divorce laws, it is encouraging to note that attitudes are changing and that judges today, in courts at all levels, are more sensitive towards gender issues and are more willing to recognize practical difficulties and address the concerns involved in each case.

In addition to a brief but thorough overview of the divorce laws in India, I have included essential practical things to remember while going through a separation and divorce, what to expect from your lawyer, coping with children during divorce and the intricacies of custody laws. Finally, I have included a chapter on understanding and coping with your own emotions and dealing with being single again.

With a supportive and loving family, going through a divorce is much easier; however, more often than not, the family structure in India is one that believes in protecting the family, not destroying it. So be prepared for a battle, both in your family and in the courts. Ultimately, if it is your well-being at risk, most families will rally around and protect their own.

As you may be aware, the law in India takes its own course, so the key word (or mantra) here is *patience*. Delays, adjournments and plain screw-ups are an unpleasant fact of the

Indian legal system. So, until substantial improvements are made not just in the laws but in the system itself, you just need to tell yourself to be patient. The best advice I received from my lawyer when I filed for divorce was to put it behind me and get on with my life. That is the only thing the law books do not tell you – that after you file for divorce, it can, unfortunately, take years to conclude this chapter in your life. Though it is far easier said than done, it is the only way to remain sane and move on.

For those of us who have experienced the grief of bad marriages, curiously, there is a lot of peace to be discovered during this time (when you are waiting for the legal formalities to be over). This book assumes the decision to divorce is final and that there is no going back. I believe that during this difficult time in your life, in order to look forward, it is always a good thing to arm yourself with courage and patience, and believe it will get better. As TUT[2] puts it, 'Thoughts become things ... so choose the good ones®!' There is a lot to be said for the power of positive thinking, and this is the time you will need it the most.

Although this book is as comprehensive as possible, it is by no means exhaustive. As mentioned earlier, it is intended only as a guide for those of you who want to get out of a bad marriage. It is, so to speak, a step-by-step guide, to divorce and all the issues you need to cope with so that you can get your life back on track and to help you gain more control over it. I have included brief real-life experiences where relevant, and mentioned a few recent and important judgements to explain some legal concepts and keep the reader abreast of latest developments. Since it is legal precedent[3] that matters in this field, I felt it was an important area to cover and I have tried to make it as simple as possible. I hope you find the book useful and informative. It is not meant to be a replacement for a lawyer – so please do consult with one to undertake and sort out the legalities of your divorce.

Finally, I'd like to thank all those who helped me shape this book – Renuka Chatterjee of Roli Books, for suggesting the idea and believing I could write it; Ashok Panda, Kalpana and Ravi Masur for reading and vetting the legal portions; my father, Sukumar R. Kirloskar for endlessly reading drafts of the manuscript and for all his patience and encouragement (and to my mother for looking over his shoulder and cheering the book on); and Arvind, for holding my hand through it all. And to all the people in this world whom I love – a very big thank you for being there for me through this very difficult period in my life – and especially to my two wonderful boys, Kartik and Raghav, for their complete support, understanding and love. It's been a great journey of self-discovery[4].

March 2007
New Delhi

Leela Kirloskar
leela.kirloskar@gmail.com

ENDNOTES

1 *India Today*, 4 December 2006. The first half of this paragraph contains information on statistics from the newsmagazine.

2 Totally Unique Thoughts®, *Reminders of Life's Everyday Magic* at www.tut.com.

3 The Wikipedia, The Free Encyclopedia defines precedent as: 'In law, a precedent or authority is a legal case establishing a principle or rule which a court may need to adopt when deciding subsequent cases with similar issues or facts. The term may also refer to the collective body of case law which a court should consider when interpreting the law. When a precedent establishes an important legal principle, or represents new or changed law on a particular issue, that precedent is often known as a landmark decision.' http://en.wikipedia.org/wiki/precedent.

4 And just in case you're wondering, I'm still waiting for that divorce to come through – it's been three years now – with no end in sight!

1

So You've Decided You Want a Divorce

To believe in tomorrow
Is to believe in yourself!
And it is stronger than
Your own destiny.

– Felipe Isaac Azofeifa (Costa Rican poet)

In many ways, the decision to divorce is easier than the myriad practical details that are sure to swamp you later. So when you know for sure this is the path your life is to take, for most people the question arises: what next?

Divorce is a scary word. It creates a highly charged atmosphere that is tense, emotional, shadowed with suspicion and bitterness, and packed with unpredictable patterns of behaviour. There are complex issues that need to be handled with sensitivity and tact but when there are a host of roller-coaster feelings that are involved, making any sort of practical decision about the break-up can be harrowing.

For most Indian men and women, families will step in, to hinder or to help, as the case may be. Of course, the level of involvement depends on whether and how strongly they support the choices you have made. All too often, making a life-changing decision like divorce means that equations shift in other relationships as well. It will impact your whole life and it is difficult for parents to take a back seat and let you make the journey on your own. And of course, there's a lot here that depends on how long you've been married, the extent of the problems that caused you to decide you want a divorce, how you are handling the break-up and whether or not you have children.

So, if you want to be in control of decisions that are ultimately going to involve you, your children (if you have any) and your life, this is the time to understand that you need to figure things out depending on what works best for you. There are some hard choices to be made, in addition to a host of practical issues that need sorting out. There is also a new life that you will build. It isn't easy and it starts here.

You can tell yourself that you have already gone through the most difficult phase, that is, making the decision to go in for a divorce. Your friends or family may have been involved in helping you reach that decision, though ultimately, this is a very personal choice. I have heard many people repeat a cliché that seems to best fit this experience and that is, *only the wearer of the shoe knows where and how much it pinches*. It is a fact that it is hard to actually break away and begin afresh. There is little doubt that despite who made the decision to divorce, it is a very difficult, deeply upsetting and painful time for both spouses.

Emotionally bruised and vulnerable people do not make the best decisions for themselves, so it is a good idea to know what you are going to be in for so that you can make informed choices to ensure a secure future. Some points below will help you take stock of your life and what steps to take subsequent to your decision.

WHO DECIDED?

Starting right from the beginning may sound terribly simplistic but it actually helps to understand how to take the next step. There are a couple of assumptions I am going to make here and the very first is that if you decided you want out, you're the one who is going to pack your bag and leave the marital home. However, there are some riders to this. One is that if you own the house, it is safe to assume that you will be the one asking your spouse to leave. If you don't, then you are the one who will leave the home. If you own it jointly, then there are some decisions to be made as to who is the one elected to leave, as well as what is going to be done to the house (who will continue to live there, will you sell it and divide the proceeds, or rent it out and share that since you may have painful memories of living there). If the house you are both living in is a rented accommodation, who stays and who moves out would quite obviously depend on who pays the rent. If you share the rent then obviously you need to sit down and decide who is going to stay and who is going to move out. In any of these situations, a fair decision can be reached with some discussion; if necessary, include close members of your family to help you.

Another extremely important factor in this initial step is how the final decision was taken (and, of course, why it finally was). The maturity of the actual separation will depend on this. Considering what an emotional issue divorce is, the probability of a peaceful break-up is low. Considering also what a dramatic lot we Indians are, the probability of melodrama and high-pitched demands for credit cards et al. to be returned is high. So your choices are limited. Pack your bags in peace with your soon to be ex-spouse looking on with a hang-dog expression, handing you your most treasured possessions, or pack them in haste and leave, with just your personal belongings! Either way, material things will be the last thing on your mind, getting out of the marital home (or getting your spouse out) the foremost.

Though it is a traumatic experience for both of you, it is a fact that the person making the decision to divorce has an easier time getting over the grief. This is because you have dealt with difficult issues during the decision-making time and put most of them behind you. At this point you will find yourself concentrating on practical issues, taking a deep breath and moving forward. As I've said earlier, it is a traumatic time for both spouses when emotions run high and both are in a vulnerable state. If something can go wrong it will, and there's no point expecting any cooperation from your spouse. You've both shut each other out of your lives, so your emotional crutches will have to be found elsewhere, or within, to get you through and out of this phase in your life. Coping isn't easy but it is important to believe that you *will* get through this time; emotionally bruised and battered, yes, but finally in one piece if you have the determination to see it through.

So, if you are the one asking your spouse to leave the house, be prepared for a tense experience during the physical moving of possessions. The more there is to pack, the longer it is going to take, especially if there is furniture to be shifted, etc. Whether you are willing to help with the practical details of the move or whether your spouse will allow you to, is another personal issue and will take some discussing. Nevertheless, you may need to offer some assistance and if you can do that in as detached manner as possible, not letting your bad experiences with him/her get in the way, it will go a long way to ensure a peaceful separation. Arjun[1], who let his ex-wife take all the furniture in their house, offered initial financial help, and even helped her to put up paintings in her new home with the hope that if she settled into her changed status without too much difficulty, it would be easier for them both through the period of waiting for their divorce to come through (as well as less trauma for their two children). Of course, the best intentions can go haywire but a mature approach to this traumatic event may help to soothe feathers, even though only temporarily.

WHAT DO YOU TAKE WITH YOU?

In most instances, this will mean primarily your personal belongings. I am not including a list here but try and imagine things beyond just your clothes and valuables – books, music, photographs and other personal mementos. This can be a difficult and painful exercise. If you are lucky, your spouse will not make an issue out of petty belongings. But if you remember what I said at the beginning of this chapter – behaviour tends to be unpredictable of even the most sensible person. So, if you can do without that gold-rimmed porcelain coffee set, leave it behind. You'll have to ask yourself how much friction you want to encounter in this, the final act of separation. For Madhu and Akash, who were married seven years, it was a simple divide of Akash keeping all the furniture, which belonged to his family, and Madhu keeping all the household items, which she had bought over the years. It can be that simple. On the other hand, Siddharth told his ex-wife to take whatever she wanted to, and only to leave his music and books alone! It all depends on how you both want to handle it. While communication is the key to handling this issue maturely, not everyone is able to view this the same way.

Important documents that you need to include in your luggage are your passport, bank locker keys and record, your cheque book(s), PPF savings account passbook if you have one, your PAN card, voter ID, credit cards, debit/ATM cards, insurance certificates, property deeds, and other financial documents like bonds and shares that are in your name. Check to see where your income-tax file is and whether you need to carry it with you. You'll need the details contained in it when you file for divorce. If you hold a joint account make sure that you keep the details so that it can be sorted out and divided later. If you own the house jointly, ensure you keep a copy of these records with you. You may have copies of police complaints in the event of domestic violence; keep those with you too. Personal documents would include health records birth certificates, educational certificates, pictures your children drew for you, letters that you can't part with photographs, cookbooks you can't do without, and other bits of nostalgia that are part of your life. Do you own your car? Then make sure your car papers and spare key are in your possession. Don't forget your marriage certificate if you have one – it is going to help you later when you file the many legal documents that are necessary for a divorce petition.

STREEDHAN: A WOMAN'S RIGHT

Streedhan is a unique concept in Hindu law and is essentially meant to ensure that a woman is entitled to keep any and all gifts that are given to her by parents, in-laws, relatives or friends at the time of marriage and throughout its duration. This includes money and jewellery. In case you have left this behind, you can later file a simple recovery suit to get back your *streedhan*. Don't forget to make a list of these items to help your lawyer. Under the Domestic Violence Act, 2005, a man cannot use his wife's *streedhan* – jewellery or clothes.

While you are going through the dozens of pieces of paper and records of the past, you are bound to come across many, many reminders of your marital life. This can be fairly distressing and depending on how you are handling things at this point, emotionally, it may be a good idea to have a close friend or relative help you sort your papers out. Don't hesitate to throw out photographs and letters if they upset you. Holding on to your past is not going to help you make a clean break for the future. If you've planned to close this chapter for good, then you have to learn to let go, no matter how painful it is. Some people do this exercise a little later, preferring to box up things and sort them out when their lives have settled down somewhat, and when they are more able to deal with this distressing task. Do what works for you and what you are comfortable with.

If you have the time, try and put away all your jewellery, other valuables and any important financial/personal documents in a locker, so that you can access them later, once your life has stabilized. This will help you to make sure you have control over them. Store the keys in a safe place or give them to someone you trust to hold them for you when you need them.

SAFEGUARD MEASURES

A good idea is to make two photocopies of all your important records and store them safely – either in a locker, or give one set to a friend to hold on to for you. This is in case you lose anything during the move. During a hostile split you won't get much help from your spouse to gather or recover these important documents.

Try to get some help while you are packing. You will have an enormous amount of luggage, even if it is just your personal possessions, and you won't be in a very stable frame of mind. It is easier to ask a close friend if you can, a parent, or a family member, for help during this difficult time. You will experience a gamut of feelings, from numbness to extreme sadness. There may be tears or rage when you are wrapping up your old life. So don't be too proud to ask for help.

WHAT ABOUT THE CHILDREN?

Later in this book there is a more detailed account of issues such as custody (that is, which parent the child/children will live with), the signs of stress in children who are traumatized by divorce, as well as dos and don'ts for parents. As far as possible, try and take decisions about the children together. This includes where they will live and how they will be taken care of. Another important issue here is telling them about the divorce. In this instance too, counsellors usually advise parents who are planning to separate and divorce to sit down and inform their children together, if they are old enough to understand it. This is, of course, the ideal way to deal with the situation. However, the reality is almost always different, and you can only handle the situation the way it is presented to you. Talking to children about a divorce between their parents is not an easy thing to do, and depending on how old they are, you can expect tears, recrimination, anger and outbursts. Some children sense what you are going to tell them after having noticed problems between both of you. This doesn't make telling them easier but in all cases, children will need reassurance from both of you about many things, so try to be as honest as you can. Telling them you love them and will be there for them even if you are divorcing the other parent will go a long way to help them feel more secure. Children need this assurance from both parents, not just one.

In India, we have the added benefit of an extended family as a support system. It's important for children to have people they love and trust around them at this time. Grandparents and uncles/aunts who they can talk to and be reassured by will help them to recover from this traumatic time faster. So don't hesitate to ask for help if you need it. It is in any case a good idea to begin to build your own support system for your children from among the people you are closest to in your life, if you don't have it already. Whether you are a mother or a father, you are going to need it, for all those times you are working, when you are tired and sometimes when you just need a break. Not surprisingly, your children need it too, mainly to reassure themselves that things are normal. Interaction with other people, rather than isolation, will help you all to bounce back that much faster.

If your children live with you, you can make things easier and more tension-free for them if you allow the other parent access whenever he/she or the children want it. This may help to avoid a nasty custody battle in court. Unfortunately, it is truer that the parent who has physical custody of the child/children will try and use this as an emotional upper hand. The huge number of custody cases filed in Indian courts, and the raucous manner in which they are contested, will attest to that. More often than not your lawyer may suggest denying your spouse access to the child/children, especially if there are fears of him/her taking the children away from your custody – kidnapping, in other words. Often, denial of access to a child is also used to pressurize the husband to cough up financial support. Although this may be a strategic tactic suggested by your lawyer, only you can decide whether it is necessary. It would obviously depend mostly on the circumstances, the prevalent hostility between you and your spouse, and finally of course, on what your children want if they are old enough to decide, or, alternatively, what would be good for them. Either way, it would have to be a careful decision, certainly not a hasty one to get back at your spouse.[2] Difficult though it may seem, it is important to keep the well-being of your child uppermost in your mind despite the many odds you may face in the ongoing battle for divorce.

While the importance of both parents remaining involved in their children's lives cannot be stressed enough, there may be situations where this becomes impossible or difficult, especially if the parent who has custody relocates to another city. If you can both sit down and decide on a temporary visitation schedule and financial support that is convenient and meets the children's needs, it would also assuage the tension and uncertainty they will feel. Of course, this is only possible when there is no hostility between the spouses, or if a cordial relationship has been arrived at for the sake of the children. You can also use the help of a family member to mediate in such a situation; parents, brothers, sisters or even an aunt or uncle who is able to talk to both of you and help you come to some agreement about the children. Even the best intentions often go awry though, as egos may get in the way, which is something you need to prepare yourself for.

Whether your children live with you or their other parent, the main thing to remember here is their comfort and needs. Which one of you can provide that is the question that needs to be addressed. A divorce is tough enough for an adult to handle. A child will be confused, upset, and angry and will need love, assurance and security from both parents. A move in such circumstances is difficult for children. If they are too young to understand what is going on (in the case of babies or toddlers, for instance) then, unquestionably the mother is the best person to have custody. However, if they are old enough to understand what is going on, it may be a good idea to ask them what they want and where they want to live. Children remember and appreciate honesty. A more forthright manner would also assure them that you are in control of your life, at least, in their eyes. As I mentioned earlier, you need to keep in mind what is best for them. Big factors to consider for you here would be your financial position and where you plan to live. For a woman, if you plan to move back to your parental home, their support and infrastructure could be a big help, at least initially.

If the children are going to live with you, and you are moving out with them, then do remember to include their health records, school records, birth certificates, etc, along with their toys and games. Try involving them while packing their clothes, as there may be a favourite toy, or even a pet they absolutely can't leave behind. Treat their needs with sensitivity as they will be confused and upset – you need to remember that they are going through a hard time too.

WHAT ABOUT YOUR FINANCES?

This is an area that tends to get neglected when one is going through an emotional upheaval. Depending on how much time you have had to decide about the divorce, or whether it is something decided in a hurry, you still need to ensure you are able to look after yourself. Your finances are going to be more important than you think, something that at this point most people will forget or treat as a minor problem in the larger scheme of things. I would suggest that you should be fully aware of how much money you've got. Reality tends to bite sooner than later and it is always better to be prepared. This is also an area which can be misused – be prepared if you don't want your account cleaned out (don't leave blank cheques lying around), records fudged, cash or jewellery swiped (yes, it happens), or your bank lockers frozen. A vindictive or selfish former partner is not going to hold back any punches, no matter how long you were married or what the quality of your married life was. So be careful. It's always safer to be aware of what might happen. After all, it's your financial health at stake.

If you are a working woman, then you already know what you are getting every month and where it's going. More often than not, in urban India, women who have opted for a divorce suddenly find themselves at the deep end when it comes to handling finances for the first time and flounder, finding it easier to hand over the responsibility to a father or brother. There is no doubt that while you are going through the initial difficult days of a separation you will hardly have the time to look into your finances. However, do try and keep tabs on things like your bank balance and other important means of saving. You may have the security of moving to your parent's home for a while until you find your feet. In this case, you have the luxury to give yourself a breather and then reassess what you need to do. This may include asking for a raise, changing jobs, deciding where you are going to live and understanding your finances better. For a woman, looking for a financial adviser or chartered accountant to help is a good idea; so don't hesitate to ask for help or advice from friends and family to find them. There is a lot of satisfaction in being able to handle your money matters yourself. Once you know your financial situation, you will find it easier to make independent decisions. Your spouse may or may not help you out – it depends upon the level of communication and the maturity with which the break-up occurs. While financial support is certainly a plus, unfortunately in India it is dependent upon a number of things, primarily whether or not your spouse is a decent human being to offer it to you. If he isn't, then you can be prepared for a long, tedious battle for that mother of all divorce issues – *maintenance*.

The law provides for an Indian woman (or man, according to Hindu law) to be maintained (that is, given financial support, either weekly or monthly) during the time they are separated or waiting for a divorce to be granted under the applicable law (see Chapters 3 and 4). However, it doesn't say how much you are entitled to and that varies from case to case, depending on the circumstances and facts involved. For this you need to sit down with your lawyer, to understand what your rights and obligations are and what you are entitled to under the law (see Chapter 2). You can file for maintenance as soon as you move out if you like, though for most people it takes a while before they get around to doing this and usually file it along with the divorce petition. Maintenance or financial support is granted from the date you file the petition – which means if it takes a few months (or years, unfortunately) to be granted, you can be assured that you are not losing out on anything as it will be paid as an accumulated amount from when you first approached the court for it (though of course, it doesn't tell you how to deal with the monthly bills while you're waiting for it!).

If you are lucky enough to be able to discuss a divorce amicably with your spouse, then in all probability you will both talk about some sort of financial package too. Also, if there are children who are living with you, then you need to discuss their needs as well – including school fees, living and clothing expenses. Try and put these decisions down in writing if you can since it's not a good idea to imagine that things will always go smoothly. There is always scope for a breakdown of any understanding you may reach, purely because of underlying hostility or bitterness. Emotions rule, so keep a hard copy of any 'friendly' agreement you may reach with your spouse; it will help should you eventually have a contested divorce, or even when filing for divorce by mutual consent.

ADD UP YOUR EXPENSES

It is a good idea to make a list of what your expenses are going to be and how you are going to be able to meet them – either via your salary, investments, or perhaps even loan. Include everything you can think of, even small items like newspaper bills – it all adds up to a fat total at the end of every month. Decide what you absolutely need and can't do without (like expensive freshly ground coffee!), and what you can let go if you really have to (like eating out thrice a week, splurging on a new gadget or having an expensive facial every month). Another golden rule is to learn to Do-it-Yourself (DIY)! Saves a ton of money and provides a whole lot of satisfaction and sense of achievement.

WHERE ARE YOU GOING TO LIVE?

If you have moved out, chances are that you have already figured this one out. It may be with your parents, temporarily, or at a friend's house until you can find a place of your own. Again, if someone is offering to help you at this point, don't let your pride get in the way. You will need all the help you can get before you get back on your feet, so there is nothing wrong in accepting a generous gesture like a temporary place to stay. Rents are phenomenally expensive in the metro cities and until you can either separate joint property, or have more control over your resources, rest assured that you will feel like a bit of a nomad for some time – perhaps even for a few years. The bottom line is to be prepared for changes in the way you are going to live until you can have some sort of permanency. Remember what I said at the beginning of this book – you need patience!

If you are looking for a place to rent, then do look at the property sections in newspapers, or talk to a broker to find out where you'd like to live and what you can afford. You may need to keep in mind the distance to your place of work and children's school when you are deciding this. Take the help of your parents and siblings. They need to know you are going to be all right, so involve them in your decisions. For a newly single woman, it is often hard to find a good landlord willing to rent out their house or apartment and it may work to take along a male relative or friend with you for moral support and to help discuss the lease, etc.

If you are going to be moving to your own place, then make a list of items you are going to need, after assessing what you already have. You may need to buy new furniture and/or stock your entire kitchen. Concentrating on something constructive often helps to take away the pain and grief that is part and parcel of such a move.

And finally, if you keep the house and your spouse moves out, it's a good idea to do some serious spring cleaning – the works if you can afford it: fresh paint, upholstery, mattresses and even beds. If money is an issue, there's a lot you can do with just soap, water and brushes – clean, clean, clean! A complete overhaul will give you a feeling of not just satisfaction, but also dust off the cobwebs of vibes that you don't want around any more. You may get stuck with a whole lot of junk that is left behind, dirty toiletry bottles and jars, old clothing, bits and pieces that you don't even want to see any more because it reminds you of your spouse – either return it to him/her, or just throw it all out. Your house is going to be your sanctuary now – you need to be comfortable in it and put your signature on it.

ARE YOU WORKING?

For a woman who has been a dependent wife and who has never worked during her married life either because she didn't need to, or because she wasn't allowed to (yes, that still happens in this country, though it seems things are set to change with the Domestic Violence Act of 2005, which provides that a man can't forcibly prevent his wife from taking up a job, or even force her to leave one), this is a time of serious reflection about your abilities and possible re-entry into the workspace. It may be a return to a profession that was given up in lieu of marriage, or to wringing out the best from the degree you earned. If you have no professional qualifications, don't worry, there's plenty you can do – you just need to look around and decide what you can handle. So this is the time to find your feet, dust off those qualifications if you have them and begin to look for a job. Decide what you can handle, the hours that you are comfortable with, who will help to look after your children when you are away, and what sort of salary you would be comfortable with. For a first-timer, working outside the home can be fairly intimidating – grit your teeth and hang in there. Added to this is the fact that you are newly separated, something you may not want to advertise. I was told by a friend once that your new civil status does not need to be hidden, nor does it need to be advertised. Perhaps that will help you to settle into your new life and all its changes. If you have the advantage of living with your parents, even temporarily, and you don't have any qualifications, then it is time to think about going back to a professional or vocational school and earning a degree/diploma to be independent in the future. Focus on your life and where you see it in the future; if you didn't before then it is time to start now.

A man's work life may not be impacted as much as a woman's – however, there will be different issues to deal with which may affect the way you work. Some of these include difficulty making decisions at the workplace, low motivation levels, distraction, anger or depression. These problems are usually temporary, but it's not a bad idea to get some counselling (if your company offers it, or privately). Financial ups and downs may also occur, depending on what your circumstances are and whether you decide to offer some financial support to your spouse.

Work can almost act like therapy, so it is not uncommon to find that you may completely immerse yourself in your work to the exclusion of all else, during this time. You need to be careful to maintain a balance, and not shut out your children, your friends and other family members who may be concerned about your well-being.

For those of you who are already settled professionally, this may be a good time to introspect and figure out whether you want to continue in your present job, or move on and change jobs. If your separation has meant that you've changed cities then you will need to network and/or look for something new. In many ways, opting for a divorce often results in a complete change in your life. This may not necessarily be a bad thing. So take the time to think about all your options, keeping in view your new civil status.

WHO ARE YOUR FRIENDS?

For too many of us, this is the time during which you will find out, sadly, who your real friends are. And the only ones whom you can count on as your friends are those who genuinely wish you well, those who will stay in touch out of real concern and those who you can turn to when you need a shoulder to cry on. You can drop the others before they drop you. Though attitudes are changing and divorce is largely becoming an accepted norm, there are still many people out there who unfortunately view it as a change (read 'drop') in status; for others it is only something new to gossip maliciously about. Yes, your so-called friends can be cruel. Radha, who had a close group of friends, who were also friends with her spouse, was shocked to learn that they knew about the problems in her marriage from her spouse, several years before she did. It's not surprising that post her separation, she decided not to see them any more.

So, don't be surprised to find yourself isolated for a while, with little socializing to speak of. It is in any case a time for introspection, so it's not such a bad thing to be on your own for a while. The family may step in to breach this gap for many – whether to share a simple cup of tea, help you work out your life, or accompany you to a movie. For others, it is a matter of picking up the pieces, moving on with a new life, a new job and, yes, finding new friends.

It is better to accept human nature and move on – you can't change what people think but your attitude towards how to handle your life will speak volumes about the kind of person you are. So it's really up to you, whether your life is going to be controlled by a peer group that really has made no real contribution to your life (emotionally speaking), or whether you plan to now live life on your own terms. In any event, you will find that most of the time you are going to be making your own decisions about your life in the future. So don't expect anyone to be holding your hand. If you can count on just a couple of close friends who enrich your life, you are very lucky to have kept them.

WHAT ABOUT COUNSELLING?

Divorce affects people in different ways. I've talked about coping with emotions during separation and post divorce in more detail in the final chapter of this book. For many people the mental anguish and pain may be so severe, debilitating or even destructive, that counselling is a serious option that must be considered. Some of you may have visited a marriage counsellor prior to your decision to divorce, to try and save the marriage, so you are already aware of what to expect. While talking about your private life may be difficult, counsellors are trained to help you to talk about what is troubling you and help find solutions that work for you. Often, expressing your grief or unhappiness helps to unlock the knot that is inside and a good counsellor will then help you on your way to a constructive recovery.

To find a counsellor, talk to friends and relatives, or check out the neurological wing (for either a clinical psychologist or just a counsellor) in a good hospital and make an appointment

Γhe number of sessions can vary, and are somewhat expensive from Rs 500-1,000 per visit). You will probably feel very ıervous during the first visit, as well as drained at the end of a particularly in-depth session, but in the end it will be a cathartic experience. Fortunately, we live in times when seeking therapy s no longer as much of a stigma as it was considered earlier. The point is that you must approach it with an open mind and give it a chance to help you. Often, it is a good way to understand the issues that led to the break-up, giving you clarity and the ability to put them at rest once and for all, in the past where they belong.

.RE YOU EATING?

Finally, the importance of looking after yourself during this ifficult phase in your life can't be stressed more. So, remember o eat meals on time, don't skip them because you are too busy r too tired or just plain 'not hungry'. You will need all the fuel ou can get for the energy you have to spend on your new life. Try and do some regular exercise – it will help to keep your pirits up. Whether you go for a walk, try yoga, or hit the gym beat your stress depends on what you are comfortable with. . lot of people turn to various support systems to get them ırough this difficult phase – whether it is getting in touch with our religion, Reiki, Buddhist chanting groups or looking for olutions through the Art of Living, Feng Shui and Vaastu – it normal and human to search for answers, so do what works for you and what you feel good about. Getting enough sleep i also equally important. Not dwelling on past hurts, anger an pain will help you to make a fresh start and think about all th things you need to do in your new life and give you impetus t tie up all those loose ends.

One of the most important things to remember is not to b too hard on yourself – so don't punish yourself unnecessarily. I the beds are not made, or the dishes piled up, or your wor papers are lying all over your dining table, it's okay. You have lot to deal with at this time, so little things like housework ca be set aside if you are going completely crazy juggling work an children in a given day. Fortunately, in India we have a lot c support in terms of service providers like maids and cooks, s this is not a lasting problem, or an insurmountable one. Try t keep it all in perspective and not spend agonizing moment wondering how to handle it all. You're only human, and thing can go wrong, it's important to remember that.

And for every good milestone in your new life – a new jol organized accounts, or just a good day, go ahead – take a da off, go shopping, head for a massage, share a frothy hazelnu cappuccino with a friend, or a day at the spa for a well-deserve pampering! You deserve it.

ENDNOTES

1 All names have been changed to protect privacy.

2 See Chapter 5, Children and Divorce, for more on this discussion.

2

You and Your Lawyer

A straight path never leads anywhere except to the objective.

– Andre Gide

You may now have been separated from your spouse for over several months or even a year or two. During this time you will have hopefully settled down into your new single life and perhaps even be ready for a fresh new life with another partner. There are loose ends to be tied up though, and you will realize that you need a divorce, in order to move on in life. Many people prefer to procrastinate, recognizing the need to get it over with but are reluctant to move ahead, as it is a complex and time-consuming process. Sooner or later, however, it is something you have to put into motion in order to put a logical end to the marriage.

Divorce in India has no DIY solutions[1], unfortunately – you need to hire a lawyer. So, the first thing you have to do is identify a lawyer to advise you on the steps to take which will help you to legally end your marriage. You will learn that there are two ways of obtaining a divorce, either in an amicable manner (divorce by mutual consent[2]), or by filing for divorce under one of the grounds available to you under the applicable law (called a contested divorce). Your lawyer will explain the intricacies of both kinds of divorce to you and will also tell you your options, depending on the facts and circumstances in your situation.

Factors to take into account here include whether there is any communication between you and your spouse. If there is, you may be able to reach a mutual understanding to visit a lawyer together and come to an amicable arrangement to end the marriage without too much agony on either side. If you are on your own, then of course, you need help to first find yourself a lawyer who will protect your interests, explain the nuances of the law and tell you what to really expect.

HOW DO YOU FIND A LAWYER?

There are many ways you can find a lawyer you will be comfortable with. Start by asking friends and family. This will ensure that you get some feedback as to the lawyer's reputation and competence. You could also ask your co-workers whether they have had any experience with a good divorce lawyer. It may be that you are referred to a lawyer whose area is not divorce law, but he/she should be able to suggest a colleague to you who has experience in family laws. If you are completely clueless about where to find one, or are too shy to ask, then you could always get on to the Net and go to Indian legal web sites[3]. If you've been to a marriage counsellor earlier, then you could even ask him/her to refer a good lawyer to you.

Finding a lawyer through referral though will give you some idea about other people's experiences so it is probably a better way to identify one in this manner. People are generally very happy to assist in referring others so you should be able to find a lawyer (or two) quickly. You may identify more than one person through other people's suggestions and your own efforts – if so, then by all means go ahead and meet the ones on your shortlist, so that you can gauge for yourself the level of comfort you feel with that person. Before your meeting, find out as much as you can about the lawyer, where he/she practices and what sort of experience your friend or colleague may have had with the person in question. Most lawyers don't charge any fees for the first meeting, so you are free to decide whether you'd like to go back and retain him/her to represent you.

What can you expect during the first meeting?

The first time you meet a lawyer may be intimidating, if only for the reason that you will be discussing your personal life with a stranger and that it may soon become part of the public domain. You are going to be a client for months certainly, possibly several years, so you need to know quickly whether or not you will be comfortable with him/her. He or she will want to know what your objective is – which is a divorce – and why. So, you will initially need to provide some background information. How much you decide to tell the lawyer at this initial meeting is up to you. I would suggest a brief sketch – an outline of your problems and the reasons for which you have decided you want a divorce. The details can be given at a later stage, once you decide that this lawyer is the right person to represent you.

The lawyer may take notes and ask you brief questions about the marriage and your problems. He or she will also want to know right away the manner in which you got married, that is, the actual ceremony and the law under which your marriage was legalized, and where (in which city/state) you got married. The law under which you got married is the same one that will apply to you for the divorce, so this detail is important, as there are different provisions under each of the personal laws that exist in this country[4]. Don't hesitate to answer the lawyer's questions in as much detail as you've decided to give at this point. If you are not comfortable with sharing anything deeper, say so clearly. He/she is asking for information only so that you can be informed of your legal options.

Questions to ask your lawyer

Once your side of the story has been narrated and the lawyer has absorbed the issues clearly, you are free to ask your own questions about the legal process. Some of the essential things you'd probably like to know right away are:

- How quickly can I file for divorce?
- What documents does the lawyer require?
- What are the grounds of divorce available to me and what do they mean?
- Where and in which court do I file for divorce?
- What are the documents that will be filed?
- How long will it take?
- How expensive will it be?
- Can I obtain an amicable divorce?
- What about custody?
- Do I get any monetary support?
- How messy can I expect it to get?
- What are my rights?
- Has he/she handled many divorce cases before?

Besides these questions, you may have others of your own that pertain to the facts of your case. Don't hesitate to ask for any clarifications right now. This is what will help you to decide if the lawyer you are talking to is the right person to handle your case. A good lawyer will give you at least an hour or more of his/her time at the first meeting to discuss your case, to enable you to decide whether you will allow him/her to handle it. He/she should be able to clearly explain the answers to all your questions and may even share some examples of recent cases (legal precedent) to help you to understand the law and its implications with respect to your divorce.

If you think that the lawyer doesn't have enough time for you, or is not giving you clear answers, then it is time to say goodbye and go to the next one on your list. Don't feel obliged to continue if you are not comfortable. As I said earlier, this is an association that will involve complex procedures and will continue at the very least for several months and may run into several years. If you feel that your lawyer is easily accessible, willing to explain things to you, affordable, and honest, and if you are comfortable in sharing the intimate details about your marriage with him/her, then you can probably go ahead and work well together.

How much is this going to cost?

For the anxious petitioner (that's you; a petitioner is the one who approaches the court for relief) this is the most important question, as finances will be foremost in your mind. I've already said earlier that this is an association that is going to take time – perhaps several years. It can't be helped, as our complex legal system is notorious, above all, for its delays. What you can do is work out how you are comfortable with paying.

A lawyer's fee depends on several factors; primary among them is the quality of the lawyer (his/her standing in legal circles), his/her seniority, and the circuit he/she is in – district or high court level, and perhaps the complexity of the case.

This determines what fees will be charged in the first instance. You can then ask your lawyer how it may be paid – in two or more installments. Fees can be paid on filing the petition (that is, your case before the court), during the time the case is heard before the court and then when you receive your decree (the pronouncement) of divorce. A silver lining here is that you can (and must) ask for legal costs (or the fees owed to your lawyer) in your petition and, depending on how convinced the judge is, you will normally get some relief. Cases where a fee is paid each time the lawyer appears in court are not unheard of. The Indian legal system today ensures that court hearings will carry on for several months and years before your divorce is resolved – you can't avoid this. What you can be careful about is the fee structure agreement you enter into with your lawyer. Often, paying the fee in installments, as long as the fee is reasonable, makes sense. You will need to be careful that your lawyer, in such an instance, isn't taking you for a ride. If the fee is reasonable per hearing (such as Rs 1,000-2,000), and payable on an 'effective' hearing (and not when your lawyer reaches court to find that the judge is holiday), you can rest assured you are in sensible hands. Do keep in mind the other factors mentioned earlier – the parameters for the fees in the first instance, before deciding what is reasonable for you and what you feel comfortable with.

Your lawyer fees in the present day (2007) should cost you

between Rs 5,000 to Rs 50,000. For instance, if you are filing a mutual consent divorce petition and you require a relatively junior lawyer to file the motion (the petition) in court and follow up on it, it may even cost you as little as Rs 3,000 (or as much as Rs 25,000 for a more experienced lawyer). Go ahead and negotiate if you are uncomfortable with the fee – it's perfectly acceptable to do that. If you can convince your lawyer that finances are a bit tight then he/she should ordinarily reduce the fee. The amount I've specified has been taken as an average, which is why I've put a ceiling to it – and despite the time taken to finally get the decree of divorce, it should not go above this ceiling. There will also be a court fee involved, which is usually minor (a few hundred rupees) and can be worked into the fee agreement.

STEP TWO

Once you've made a decision about retaining your lawyer, and got the expenses out of the way, you will have to make time for a longer meeting, as this is when you will decide on the strategy of how to obtain the divorce. He/she will first tell you that you have two options, or ways in which you will be able to get your divorce. These are:

- Divorce by mutual consent
- Contested divorce

By mutual consent[5]

Here, the effort is to find an amicable solution and conclusion to the marriage, what is termed a no-fault divorce. There is a legal provision for mutual consent divorce in all the personal laws in India, following various amendments to the laws that were made over the years. Your lawyer will ask you whether it is possible to talk to your spouse to settle the matter amicably. He/she may suggest, before you take the discussion further, to try to talk it out with your spouse and come to some mutual agreement. This effort to resolve the marriage amicably can be done either by you or your lawyer. It entails either (by you or your lawyer) a phone or face-to-face conversation with your spouse, informing him/her that you would like a divorce and whether he/she would like to sit down and resolve it amicably. This is a sensible, mature option, as it is faster and cleaner for both of you. So, if you can make a last-ditch effort at discussing a divorce by mutual consent, by all means do so. Your lawyer can then step in to help you negotiate a financial settlement (for a woman), which is usually (and preferably) made as a one-time lump sum payment.

A petition under mutual consent is a simple one to prepare and can be prepared by one or both of you and contains just the details of your marriage, the fact that you've both agreed you want a divorce, the custody and financial agreement you have both entered into with regard to the children if any, and the financial settlement that has been made to the wife. If you face hostile or uncooperative behaviour (which often occurs during negotiations, especially when the financial settlement is discussed) to file for a divorce under this easy provision, give yourself a time frame within which you tell yourself you will go ahead and file for divorce under the grounds available to you (that is, a contested divorce) if nothing works out. It is also the fastest way to get a divorce in India today, as the courts have now held that the waiting period of six months (the process includes two motions of divorce, one after a year of separation and the second six months following the first motion, before the divorce can be granted) can be done away with if the marriage is well and truly over. A divorce by mutual consent is discussed in detail in the following chapter.

Contested

If you have no option but to go in for a contested divorce, it means you will be filing a petition in the relevant court (called a fault divorce) under one of the grounds for divorce spelt out in the law that applies to you. In this case, your lawyer will first note the details for drafting and filing your divorce petition clearly and create a file for you. In addition to some of the information I've mentioned earlier, you will also need to provide him/her with various details and photocopies of documents including:

- Your income tax (IT) statements for the previous 2-3 years (for the judge to decide on maintenance or financial support if you require it, and to support your request).

- Your current employment, salary and some work history.
- Your date of birth, place of birth, and the names of your parents.
- The names of your children if any, and their dates of birth.
- Your current residence and how long you've been there; whether it is rented or owned.
- Any other source of income.
- Details of property or other assets, if any, owned by you.
- Whether your spouse is giving you any financial support; if yes, the details; if not, why not?
- Whether any communication with your former spouse exists; if so is it amicable or hostile?
- Where do your children live? With you, your spouse or their grandparents? Where do they go to school and who pays for their education and other requirements?
- What are your fixed expenses (usually listed in a petition requesting for maintenance under the applicable law, again to help the judge decide what you should receive)?
- Any other information relevant to the divorce, such as a list of your spouse's income and assets and lifestyle (for instance, does he/she have credit cards, travels abroad often, club memberships and number and make of car/s).

All this information will go towards drafting your divorce

petition – the document by which you approach the appropriate court asking for a divorce on the grounds stated therein. Your lawyer will also note details about your spouse, including his/her date of birth, parents' names and where he/she currently resides. If you can provide some employment and financial information about him/her, it would help your lawyer too – so be prepared to make lists of credit cards, property, bank accounts, etc. These details are mainly required by women to be noted in the maintenance petition when seeking financial support, but could be collected by a man too, to show that he doesn't need to support his wife as she's quite capable of supporting herself.

RIGHT TO INFORMATION

The Right to Information Act, 2005, empowers you to ask for information in government records. It can be particularly useful in gathering financial information about your spouse such as property ownership, company ownership, etc. Look up the web site www.rti.gov.in to find out how to obtain the information you need and where to file for it.

And finally, you will need to give your lawyer a detailed histor of your marriage – when and where you were married, an everything that happened thereafter, leading to the separatio and the decision to divorce. This part is difficult because yo will need to give him/her all the sordid details that led to you break-up. Since this is your lawyer you can't leave out anything – it is best to be as honest as possible, since he/she is going to advise you on your options how to legally end the marriage. Lawyers are required to keep the details of their clients confidential; if you aren't sure, ask – your lawyer will oblige the request to protect your privacy. Also, it may be easier if you remember that lawyers handle hundreds of such cases regularly and are usually desensitized to the most delicate issues involved – so there's nothing they haven't heard before. It's a little like a woman going to the gynaecologist for an internal check-up for the first time – you are more embarrassed than they are!

When your lawyer has understood the information he/she has been given, you will be given options as to what are the grounds for divorce under which it is most appropriate to file your case. For instance, adultery and physical and/or mental cruelty[6] are two of the most cited grounds in a contested divorce. Ask your lawyer as many questions as you like to fully understand these provisions. The facts and circumstances of your case will become part of the public record and you need to be comfortable about what you say in the petition. Unfortunately, many people wish to rip apart their spouses so the divorce petition is often a vitriolic statement that contains half-truths and sometimes, outright fabrications. Remember also that this is a civil case and may go to trial in the event you are unable to settle the issues amicably at any point in the case (which is also an option – even after you file for a contested divorce, you are free to resolve it amicably, in which case you jointly file a mutual consent petition and withdraw the earlier one, or the judge rules that both the parties have mutually come to an understanding and grants the divorce). So, how you handle the initial stage of filing statements is important, as you won't be able to retract them later.

You may also be advised to file in addition to the divorce petition:

- A petition asking for maintenance, both interim (called *pendente lite*, or financial support during the time your petition/divorce is pending in court) and final (or alimony as it is popularly known); and
- A custody petition: asking for your children to live with you, or for visitation rights, depending on the circumstances involved.

Once you've given all the details, and your petition is ready to draft, your lawyer will ask you to sign a *vakalatnama* – this authorizes him/her to appear for you in court. Ask for a photocopy to keep in your records and remember to make copies of every single piece of paper that you hand over to your lawyer. This ensures you not only have a record but in the event you need to suddenly change your lawyer for some reason, it will come in handy. In case you do decide to change lawyers, then you will have to settle his/her dues, after which you can ask for a No Objection Certificate (NOC), without which another lawyer may not represent you.

Your lawyer will now inform you that he/she is going to draft out the petition, which will be filed in the appropriate court. Once it is ready, you will be called to the lawyer's office to read and correct it if required, then sign it so it is ready to be filed. This should take no more than two weeks from the time you've given all your details to the lawyer. When you've signed the petition, the affidavits and appended additional documents that the lawyer feels are necessary at this point (for example, your IT statements and your salary slips), the lawyer's clerk will file the petition in the court and let you know on what date it will be heard. In the first instance, a notice will be given to the other side (your former spouse) as well as a copy of your petition to him/her, to appear in court and to file their rejoinder or objection statement, as it is commonly called, to your petition (which is a reply to the various statements you've made in your petition).

Be warned that in a hostile situation, even serving a notice to your former spouse may take time. More often than not, unscrupulous spouses will not hesitate to delay things, avoiding the notice several times. The court has a system where the notice will initially be sent by registered post, the second time by hand (*dasti* as it is called), and finally if both these don't work, a copy of the notice is plastered outside the house of your spouse. It is taken to mean that the notice has been served. He/she then finally has no option but to appear in court on the designated date (or suffer contempt of court). Unfortunately, this can all waste a lot of time – months and months of it.

HOW LONG WILL IT ALL TAKE?

How long is a Chinese name? Unfortunately, this is completely dependent on the vagaries of the Indian legal system as well as the efficiency of your lawyer. Paperwork takes an awfully long time to prepare and lawyers are always flooded with other cases – you may need to make several phone calls to remind your lawyer that you are waiting for the draft divorce petition, maintenance application, etc, in the event it takes more than two weeks to prepare. What you need in abundance here is patience. It is easier to make it a goal at a time. When the papers are filed, the success of the notice being delivered, the rejoinder being filed, the first hearing – all these will be milestones – and maybe far, far apart! The frustrations include when you find the judge isn't available, has changed, or the court vacations delay hearings or when the other side is determined to give you a hard time and plays games from the moment a notice is ordered to be given to them. Patience is the only way to endure the process. Between dates (and if you are lucky, you will get these a month apart), try and put it aside and get on with life.

Given the above, realistically, a 3-7-year time frame is what you can expect it will take to conclude, in a contested divorce. A lot depends upon what happens during this time. More often than not, factors like sheer exhaustion, pressures of financial payments, personal or family pressures, or even plans to remarry, may lead to an out-of-court negotiation and settlement.

DOCUMENTS TO BE FILED IN COURT

Your divorce petition comprises different documents, the main one being the petition itself. These are standard form documents that are filed in court, and they are crafted depending under what provision you file – either by mutual consent, or under one of the grounds of divorce given in the law that applies to you. They are long-winded and usually filled with legalese. When you read them before signing, if there's anything you don't understand, ask your lawyer to clarify it.

The divorce petition

This is the document that you will file in court requesting the grant of a divorce decree. It clearly states the law under which you are applying and the ground or provision under which a divorce is being sought.

PRECAUTIONARY STEPS

As a measure of abundant caution, ask for and keep copies of every document that is filed as well as any document you hand over to your lawyer.

In the mutual consent divorce petition, the parties to the divorce, that is you and your spouse, will jointly mention in brief your names, ages, details of the marriage, the reasons why the marriage has failed beyond repair and state that you both agree to a divorce without any pressures from either spouse. This document needs to be signed by both of you. As mentioned earlier, it ordinarily contains a financial settlement that has been agreed to by both sides (normally protecting the interests of the woman) and an agreement that decides where the children will live, who is responsible for their finances and how their time will be divided between the parties. Once the judge feels it is a fair settlement, that the parties mutually agree to divorce and that there is no coercion on either party to divorce, and is satisfied that the marriage has irretrievably broken down, he/she will ordinarily grant the divorce.

If you are filing a divorce petition under one of the grounds of divorce provided, it will also include all the information your lawyer took from you earlier. So, as briefly and clearly as possible it should include your details (name, age), when and where you got married, some details of your spouse, and a history of the marital discord. Particular incidents your lawyer feels are necessary to strengthen the petition will be described in some detail, to reinforce the fact that you feel the divorce is essential. This document necessarily is a fairly exhaustive one and will run into many pages. It is also the basis upon which other documents such as the application for maintenance are made. The complete factual record needs to be made here and you need to satisfy yourself that it is a true and clear account. Your lawyer will advise you as to what is absolutely necessary to make the ground for divorce under which you are filing valid. After all, this is the document based upon which the judge is going to be convinced enough to grant you a divorce. So it needs to be as watertight as possible, without making trumped up, falsified statements.

After the lengthy factual statement, there will be relief asked for – a divorce, and of course any other relief the judge would like to grant (a standard request) as well as legal costs to be granted (the other side pays – a common request if you are a woman).

Since the matter may go to trial, you need to keep in mind that you may be cross-examined on the statements you make in this petition. So whatever you say will be gone over in with excruciating detail and you may prefer to be spared any embarrassment with regard to very intimate details between you and your former spouse. A sensitive lawyer will advise you more about what details are relevant to put in and what can be left out of the petition.

Affidavits

An affidavit is essentially a one-page document that verifies what you are saying in the petition is true to the best of your knowledge. You'll need to file these with every petition that is filed in court. It is a standard form document.

Maintenance petition[7]

You may be asking for some financial support from your former spouse. This is usually in the case of women but it is not unheard of for a man to ask for monetary support from his former wife, in the event that she was the primary bread-earner. This is an area that is much abused, though, and the woman is hit the hardest. While there is no getting away from difficult spouses who don't want to pay their wives any maintenance, what is heartening, as I've said earlier in this book, is that attitudes in the judiciary are slowly changing, for the better, something that is reflected in decisions taken even by policy makers (an example is the Hindu Succession [Amendment] Act 2005, which removes the gender discrimination and grants daughters and sons the same rights to ancestral property).

The maintenance petition will contain the brief facts that are already there in your divorce petition, and then more details about your financial life. This includes your current income, your fixed expenses and further details about any assets you own (if any) and why you require financial support. In the first instance, you will be asking for maintenance in the interim period – that is, while the divorce case is pending in court. In the second instance, you will be asking for a final maintenance amount that the judge will grant, based on the information provided and also after hearing the other side.

You and your lawyer would have come to a figure after calculating what you earn and what your fixed expenses and needs are. In addition, what is taken into account are factors such as the standard of living that you have been used to (as it is not the intention for you to live a hand-to-mouth existence) and your spouse's lifestyle (if the amount you are asking for is a substantial one). The amount of maintenance asked for varies from case to case. This is a grey area in the law as no upper limit exists (it was removed following an amendment to the law several years ago). Previously very small amounts were granted as maintenance; but many judges both at the district and high court level grant more realistic amounts as maintenance. You would have filed your maintenance petition in the district courts (city civil courts), for to file in the high court you would have to declare yourself an 'indigent person' – or technically bankrupt. It is preferable to file in the district court and work your way up if required (you can appeal for an enhanced amount if you are not satisfied with what the judge grants you in the district court). So in the first instance, your lawyer should advise (sensibly) a conservative figure which would be more realistically granted. Obviously, the amount you ask for would depend on the lifestyle you are used to.

Custody petition

This petition is filed in the Guardianship and Wards Court, a designated court in the district courts – and pertains specifically to the children involved. Which parent is to have physical custody of the child/children, who is to have the financial responsibility, and the visitation rights of the other parent are decided here. The *only* consideration to the decision of the judge is the well-being of the child, which the judge will gather either from the facts contained in the petition (if the child is very young) or from talking to the child/children in chambers (the judge's office within the court complex), without anyone else present.

The custody petition will contain brief details of the divorce petition filed, details of the child/children, where they currently study and live, and who is taking care of their needs, financial and emotional. It will also contain reasons for which you believe you should have custody and states clearly that it is in the child/children's best interest that they are with you. Relief asked for is custody and/or visitation (scheduled visits during weekends and holidays, structured by you or the court, according to the child's convenience). A relevant detail here is that the Supreme Court of India held in a case in 1999 that *both* mother and father are the natural guardians of a child (earlier it was only the father); thus it follows that custody can be given to either – depending on the relevant facts and circumstances of the case and of course, what the child wants. Another interesting case was where the Supreme Court held that remarriage of the mother would not prevent her from having custody, provided the child/children wanted to be with her.

STRATEGIES

Your lawyer will advise you of the best way to file these petitions – separately or all together. Often, to increase the pressure on your spouse, they are filed one after the other. It is best to file them all separately so that one doesn't get stuck because of delays in the other (this applies to the maintenance and divorce petition). Remember that it is the notice to the other party that takes the longest time. Once that has been done, you will get your first hearing date where the other side has to file a rejoinder to your petition for divorce (as well as replies to both your maintenance and custody petitions). After this stage come the arguments, which your lawyer will make on your behalf, on which the judge will pass orders according to the relief which is requested. You may also have to appear personally in court before the judge several times. A decision should also be made in your maintenance petition at this point, if you are lucky, a few months after you file (it may take up to a year or slightly longer for the maintenance to be granted). Then, following your personal visit/s to court, issues are framed and the trial occurs, during which you may need to call family members to speak for you in court, after which the divorce will be granted.

GOING TO COURT

You may perhaps be called personally to court several times. On the very first appearance, in a contested divorce, usually the first date itself, there is a token attempt at reconciliation by the judge. This mandatory provision was made due to the attitude of the ancient law-makers towards marriage as a sacred union, to be broken only if there was no other choice (found in more than one personal law in the country). The reality today is that the judge will ask you if you really want a divorce – if you nod your head and reply clearly in the affirmative, that's the end of it.

Going to court may intimidate those who have never visited the district (or any other) courts before and who believe it to look like what is portrayed in a Hindi movie. The reality is that they are dingy little rooms which are difficult to find – located as they are in huge, untidy court complexes, with little or no ventilation, crowded, noisy corridors filled with filthy smells and spills, bad parking, nowhere to sit, and no other service to speak of. Coffee in cardboard cups may be had in the canteen and if you plan to visit the toilets – don't. The judge sits on a raised podium, and there will be a few rickety chairs and tables in front, with the court clerk, court master and recorder on either side of him/her. You may not even be allowed inside until your case has been 'called' (which they do loudly and lustily for the whole world to hear). A list of cases that will be heard on that day is tacked up on a board that is hanging on its hinges outside the door of the court room. Your first action will be to peer over the shoulders of others who are looking to see what number their case is. And then, you settle in to wait for yours to be called. You'll be doing a lot of that in the months to come. Take it all in your stride for there is a long way to go before you get your divorce.

ENDNOTES

1 British citizens, for instance, can obtain a DIY divorce in the UK, where you can choose to do all the paperwork yourself, online, including file motions in court, for a no-fault or fault divorce, where it is not contested. It is easy, fast and inexpensive, as well as less stressful.
2 Discussed in detail later in this chapter and in Chapters 3 and 4 of this book.
3 Like www.helplinelaw.com which takes queries and is very prompt in replying. I have included a few more in Useful Resources at the end of this book.
4 Given in Chapters 3 and 4 of this book.
5 Details of procedures etc, for a mutual consent divorce are contained in Chapters 3 and 4 of this book.
6 Explained in Chapters 3 and 4.
7 Legal provisions and detailed discussion contained in Chapters 3 and 4 of this book.
8 Children and Divorce is discussed in Chapter 5 of this book and contains details about custody.

3

Divorce Under Hindu Law

How poor they are that have not patience!
What wound did ever heal but by degrees?

– William Shakespeare

We live in a country that is richly diverse in nature with people of different faiths. Recognizing that each faith is unique and requires separate treatment prompted the enactment of different personal laws that govern the areas of marriage and divorce in the religious communities in India. While this was done out of respect to the different religions that prevail in India, there is a growing feeling (prompted by sporadic reminders to the government by the Supreme Court of India) that perhaps we should have a uniform civil code in accordance with a suggestion in one of the Directive Principles of State Policy in the Indian Constitution (Article 44). Such a uniform law, it is argued, would help to streamline the law and its application and help to remove the inadequacies and contradictions due to different ideologies.

There is no doubt that this is a valid suggestion and would help to greatly improve the personal laws, given that most of them were enacted so many years ago, in different social conditions. A re-look at the divorce laws would certainly simplify what is today an enormously complicated law(s) and procedure, under which it takes years to obtain a divorce and which seldom takes practical needs or gender issues into consideration. It would almost certainly reduce the backlog of matrimonial cases pending in the courts today and help to ease the process. According to an article on young divorces recently[1], 5,475 such cases (young people wanting a divorce) were filed in Delhi alone; 2,550 in Mumbai (these are figures for 2004). These figures are growing exponentially each year, with more and more people seeking their way out from bad marriages.

The laws that govern divorce in India are:

- The Hindu Marriage Act, 1955
- The Divorce Act, 1869 (earlier known as the Indian Divorce Act, 1869)
- The Dissolution of Muslim Marriage Act, 1939
- The Muslim Women (Protection of Rights on Divorce) Act, 1986

- The Parsi Marriage and Divorce Act, 1936
- The Special Marriage Act, 1954
- The Foreign Marriage Act, 1969

THE HINDU MARRIAGE ACT, 1955

Under Hindu law, marriage was a sacred, eternal and holy union between a man and a woman. The ceremony includes the *saptapadi* or seven steps, around the sacred fire, without which it is not recognized as a valid marriage. According to ancient scriptures, marriage enabled one to live a happy life, procreate and do one's duty (dharma). This dynamic law eventually recognized that not all marriages stayed happy and not all men and women did their duty. Social reformists propagated the concept of divorce which was accepted and woven into this law, which came into existence eight years after India's independence. It applies to Hindus, Buddhists, Jains and Sikhs (as well as to anyone who is not a Christian, Muslim, Parsi or Jew).

According to Section 14 of the Act, you have to be married for at least a year before you can approach the courts for a divorce. However, this provision may be relaxed in exceptionally difficult situations. Section 13(1) and (1A) of the Act provides the grounds under which either spouse can approach the appropriate court for a decree of divorce. These include:

- Adultery
- Cruelty
- Desertion
- Conversion or change of religion
- Insanity
- Leprosy
- Venereal disease
- Renunciation of world
- Presumption of death
- Non-resumption of cohabitation after passing of a decree for judicial separation
- Non-resumption of cohabitation after passing of a decree for restitution of conjugal rights.

In addition to the above, the wife is also entitled to the following four grounds for divorce:

- Bigamy/polygamy
- Rape, sodomy or bestiality
- Non-resumption of cohabitation after passing of a decree for maintenance
- Repudiation of marriage.

More about the grounds for divorce under Hindu law

Adultery

Adultery is understood to mean when a married person has

consensual (or voluntary) sexual relations with another who is not his/her spouse. It is also a criminal offence and requires a greater degree of proof under the criminal law (that is, beyond reasonable doubt). However, in matrimonial cases, although the evidence may be based on inferences and probabilities, adultery was earlier extremely difficult to establish, as some penetration[2] had to be proved. An amendment to the law in 1976 provided that one act of adultery was enough to obtain a divorce. Following this amendment, some judgements were passed which took a more reasonable view of the matter and it was held that adultery can be established by the 'preponderance of probabilities'. This means that if 'presumptive proof' is provided, or proof by which it can be presumed that adultery has occurred, by circumstantial evidence, evidence of non-access to the spouse and the birth of a child, contracting a venereal disease and/or confession or admission of the act, it is enough to prove adultery.

Cruelty

Cruelty implies conduct that is mentally or physically injurious, causing danger to life, limb or health. It is a ground for both judicial separation[3] and divorce. Prior to the 1976 amendment to the Act, cruelty was usually interpreted very rigidly as most judges believed (and still believe) that marriage was a sacrament and shouldn't be dissolved, especially for often intangible reasons (when mental cruelty was cited). Following this amendment, however, it is now recognized that for cruelty to be accepted as a ground for divorce, the conduct complained of should be so serious that the person complaining of it cannot be expected to live with the other. Important factors to show cruelty of a spouse include the facts and incidents of such behaviour viewed along with the state of the marriage and its history. Mental cruelty is to be inferred from a series of acts, not a single act.

Cruelty is not an exhaustive term, as it (both mental and physical torture) has been found in instances of[4]:

- Denial of food
- Perverse sexual conduct
- Locking a woman out of the house (not one instance but constantly)
- Denying (a woman) access to (her) children
- Constant taunts, nagging, demoralizing and putting down a woman with the intent of causing mental torture
- Confining a woman indoors and not allowing her to mix with people
- Abusing children in the presence of the mother, causing mental anguish
- Denying paternity, with the intention of causing mental pain
- Threatening divorce unless dowry is given.

Continuous ill treatment, denial of sexual intercourse, neglect, indifference (on the part of the husband), and implying the wife is unchaste are all acknowledged as behaviour amounting to cruelty. The interpretation of cruelty by the courts in a multitude of cases over the years applies to both men and women, and although it has largely been wives who have been at their husband's mercy, it is interesting to note that there are a growing number of men in recent times who have filed for divorce under this ground, citing unbearable cruel treatment by their wives. The Supreme Court recently[5] held that indifference, frigidity and abstinence from sex are also counted as cruelty.

Courts have found it more difficult to conclude cases where mental cruelty is alleged, while even a single act of physical violence is enough to amount to physical cruelty. What is clear from the many judgements that have been passed in divorces that are filed under this ground is that each case depends on its own peculiar facts and circumstances. For instance, according to a judgement of the Supreme Court of India, throwing your *mangalsutra* at your husband does not constitute mental cruelty.[6] On the other hand, impotency has been found to amount to mental cruelty.[7] If you are filing for divorce under this ground, be prepared to recall and record every instance of the cruel treatment or behaviour towards you as it will be relevant to show it was an ongoing situation and not an isolated incidence.

Desertion

If one spouse deserts or abandons the other intentionally for a continuous period of at least two years (before filing the petition), it is a ground for divorce. Desertion was explained further in the 1976 amendment as being without reasonable cause, without the consent of the other spouse as well as wilful neglect. Again, each case is decided on its own facts and circumstances.

Conversion or change of religion

In the event either of the spouses converts to or adopts another religion, he or she is no longer a Hindu. While this by itself does not dissolve the marriage, it becomes a ground for divorce. This has often been the case where a Hindu man decided to convert to Islam in order to remarry. In a leading case,[8] the Supreme Court held that while a Hindu husband has the right to convert to another religion (to Islam in this case, which permits multiple marriages) he has no right (under The Hindu Marriage Act, 1955) to remarry without dissolving his first marriage.

Insanity

If it is established that one spouse is suffering from an unsound mind or has a mental illness or psychopathic disorder that is so severe and incurable (such as schizophrenia) that the other spouse cannot possibly live with him/her, it is a ground for divorce. It is for the petitioner to prove this allegation of insanity to the court.

Leprosy

If one spouse is suffering from a 'virulent and incurable' form of leprosy, it is a ground for divorce for the other. The petitioner has to prove to the court that his/her spouse not only has leprosy but the disease is one that is 'virulent and incurable'.

Venereal disease

If the venereal disease (such as gonorrhea or syphilis) alleged is a communicable one, that is, if it can infect others who come in contact with the person infected, it is a ground for divorce.

Renunciation of world

In the event one of the spouses decides to renounce the world and enter a religious order, it is a ground for divorce, though only for the other spouse (not the one renouncing the world). Also, the declaration must be complete and final and accompanied by actually entering the religious order (and all the ceremonies that are part of such an act), not by just declaring that one is a *sanyasi*.[9]

Presumption of death

If one spouse has not been seen or heard of as alive for at least seven years, by people (including close friends and relatives) who would have 'naturally heard' of it, he/she is presumed to be dead and this becomes a ground for divorce for the other spouse. To clarify here, a decree of divorce is required to dissolve the marriage (before remarrying) and it does not mean one is a widow/widower.

Non-resumption of cohabitation after passing of a decree for judicial separation

If the spouses have not resumed cohabitation after one or more years after a decree of judicial separation has been passed (to which they were both parties), this becomes a ground for divorce. However, the spouse seeking a divorce, or the petitioner, under this ground, should not be taking advantage of his/her own wrong or disability, that is, he/she should not be the reason for which divorce was sought in the first place. There should also be no other legal reason for refusing the divorce.

Non-resumption of cohabitation after passing of a decree for restitution of conjugal rights[10]

If the parties do not comply with a decree for restitution of conjugal rights for one or more years after passing of the decree, it becomes a ground for divorce. Again, the court has to consider whether or not the petitioner is taking advantage of his/her own wrong conduct.

CONJUGAL RIGHTS

Cohabitation means that husband and wife are living together and are bound by certain marital rights and obligations called conjugal rights, including the right to the 'society' or company of your spouse, right of residence and financial support, and sexual intercourse which is an important component of cohabitation.

Bigamy

This ground for divorce is only available to the wife. It applies only to bigamous/polygamous marriages. Previously, it applied to marriages that took place before the commencement of the Act, which meant that many men got away with having second wives (a concept the scriptures, especially *Manusmriti*, encouraged, as the primary reason for marriage was to beget an heir; if the wife couldn't produce one, then the husband was entitled to marry again). Following an amendment to the law in 1976, it now applies to marriages solemnized before or after the Act, giving this clause more teeth. Bigamy is far from being an old practice – Census 2001 found evidence of up to 10 million women living in bigamous marriages.[11] Bigamy is also a criminal offence,[12] punishable with seven year's imprisonment and a fine.

Rape, sodomy or bestiality

A man is guilty of rape when he has intercourse with a woman, according to the definition given in Section 375 of the Indian Penal Code, 1860:

- Against her will.
- Without her consent.
- With her consent, when her consent has been obtained by

putting her or any person in whom she is interested in fear of death or of hurt.

- With her consent, when the man knows that he is not her husband, and that her consent is given because she believes that he is another man to whom she is or believes herself to be lawfully married.
- With her consent, when, at the time of giving such consent, by reason of unsoundness of mind or intoxication or the administration by him personally or through another of any stupefying or unwholesome substance, she is unable to understand the nature and consequences of that to which she gives consent.
- With or without her consent, when she is under sixteen years of age.

The definition adds that penetration is sufficient to constitute sexual intercourse necessary to this heinous offence. Strangely, as a contradiction to the personal laws, marital rape is *not* recognized by the Indian Penal Code – given in the exception to this definition as: 'Sexual intercourse by a man with his own wife, the wife not being under fifteen years of age, is not rape.' However, women are now protected by the new Domestic Violence Act of 2005 which provides that a man cannot sexually abuse his wife, or force sex, pornography or other obscene material on her.

Sodomy[13] or bestiality[14] is also defined in Section 377 of the Indian Penal Code as 'voluntary carnal intercourse against the order of nature with any man, woman or animal ...' These three offences are available as grounds for divorce only to the wife.

Non-resumption of cohabitation after passing of a decree for maintenance

If, after one or more years following the passing of a decree for maintenance in favour of the wife, under either the Code of Criminal Procedure, 1973, or the Hindu Adoption and Maintenance Act, 1956, the husband and wife do not resume living together, this becomes a ground for divorce, only for the wife.

Repudiation of marriage

This was a new clause inserted in Section 13 of the Hindu Marriage Act following the amendment in 1976. It means a woman can file for a divorce under this ground if she was married before the age of fifteen but repudiated or rejected the marriage before she turned eighteen. This last provision is a soft one as delays in filing such a petition for divorce have been condoned if the petitioner was not aware of her options before turning eighteen. This new provision is an indication of how progressive Hindu law has become especially for women.

THE PROCEDURE

The petition for divorce under any of the grounds explained

above is filed ordinarily in the district court in the jurisdiction (or city) where either the marriage took place, or where the petitioner lives (only if it is the wife). It can also be filed in the city where both spouses last lived together, or where the respondent lives when the petition is filed.

The petition will contain all the details that are required with regard to the facts and the relief requested, and is accompanied by an affidavit verifying the statements in the petition. You will probably prepare this together with your lawyer. Do remember to hold on to a copy of this for your records, along with the *vakalatnama*.

Once the divorce petition is filed, notice is sent to the other party directing the filing of a rejoinder to the petition. This is essentially a reply to the petition and will rebut or reply to all the points raised in the petition. Expect this stage to take some time, as more often than not delays are protracted due to the conduct of the parties to a case. A matrimonial case is no exception. If the other spouse does not respond to the court notice summoning him/her to court, the court can even proceed ex parte (that is, without the other side being present). However, this is only done once all means of sending the notice are carried out by registered post, by hand and finally, pasted outside the residence).

The court (that is, the judge) will ask for you and your spouse to be present on a given date and make an attempt at reconciliation as this is a mandate in the law. So don't be surprised if you are standing before the judge and he/she asks you whether you'd like to go back to your spouse. Your lawyer will tell you when to expect this. The judge cannot force anyone to reconcile, so this is usually a token attempt.

When the paperwork is complete (including your counter reply to the rejoinder) the issues are framed and the matter goes to trial (remember this is a civil case, therefore the Code of Civil Procedure, 1908, applies). Post this lengthy process, you can hope for a divorce. While there is a provision clearly prescribing a speedy end to the proceedings, it is an unfortunate fact that in our current overloaded legal system, delays are part and parcel of any litigation. So, it can take years before you get your divorce, depending on how messy it is.

Maintenance

There are two types of maintenance available to a spouse who does not have independent financial means. During the time the divorce case is pending in the courts, the court can grant *pendente lite* or interim expenses to the spouse who has filed for it. This is a monthly or weekly amount granted to take care of expenses during the time the divorce proceedings are continuing in court. Hindu law does not distinguish between husband and wife in this regard, and even the husband can file for maintenance if he can prove that he has no independent income. Maintenance is recognized even in the Code of Criminal Procedure, 1973 (Section 125), where prior to the amendment in 2002, the maximum amount was Rs 500 per month. Following the amendment the amount has been left to the discretion of the judge. The interim maintenance has to be provided for within sixty days (though delays, again, are routine).

Under The Hindu Marriage Act, 1955, Section 24 provides for interim expenses, on the basis of the income of either the husband or wife, as the case may be. It is normally one-third of the income and there is no upper limit. Costs incurred for the proceedings can also be requested. The court is also supposed to take into account a man's or woman's credit cards, mobile phone bills, hotel bills, income-tax returns, cars and lifestyle while granting maintenance. Section 25 provides for final alimony or maintenance, which is granted at the time of divorce as a lump sum or monthly payment.

This is an area that is greatly abused by men, who hide their incomes to avoid the payment of maintenance and the discharge of their moral responsibilities towards their spouses. In India, more often than not, a wife (especially a wife who does not work or is dependent) is not privy to the financial decisions made by the husband, and therefore has no clue as to where the income goes (often her own income as well). Having no control over it means that when she files for divorce and maintenance, she is often in a state of extreme financial difficulty. In a very recent case,[15] the Delhi High Court ruled that if a husband commits a default in the payment of interim maintenance to his wife and children, he is not entitled to a divorce in proceedings that he has filed. This progressive judgement will benefit women who are stranded financially to cope on their own by their husbands who obtain a divorce without paying the maintenance.

This provision in the law was meant to help avoid such situations, but obviously it is still an area which is not effective enough. Fortunately, in recent times, there are a growing number of instances where proactive judges (especially in high courts) have recognized practical financial realities and have awarded very decent amounts of maintenance. However, women are still not entitled to property acquired during the marriage. So in most cases, women are too exhausted to fight for their rights, or they get short-changed by their spouses. The only way to ensure a fair division of assets and finances is to have a joint account/property in joint names, during the marriage, or a prenuptial agreement, which is rare in India. Since these practicalities are rarely thought of, when a marriage breaks up, it is almost always the woman who is the loser. In the new Domestic Violence Act women have, for the first time, been given the right of residence – a man cannot sell the house in which his wife is staying; and if the house is being rented, he has to pay the rent or provide another place for her to live. A man also cannot give away his right to a property in which his wife is staying without the consent of the court[16].

Judicial separation

If a husband and wife wish to separate legally, without a divorce, they can approach the court for a judicial separation, under Section 10 of the Act. Thus, it is a way to end a marriage without the bloodshed of breaking the legal bond. The essential ingredient is that the spouses do not cohabit; in some instances – more commonly in the West than here – they may even continue to live under the same roof. In fact, in India, it is more common for couples not to approach the courts for a formal judicial separation, preferring to lead separate lives and coming to this decision amicably and quietly. You can apply for judicial separation at any time during the marriage.

Remarriage after a judicial separation would amount to bigamy and is illegal under this provision. Interestingly, however, if one of the spouses dies during the judicial separation, the surviving spouse is entitled to succeed to the property of the deceased spouse.

Restitution of conjugal rights

Another archaic provision that is impossible to execute is a decree of restitution of conjugal rights. It says that in the event one spouse abandons the other without a valid reason, the other spouse can seek relief under this provision. It is, however, impossible to compel or force someone to live with another. The law provides that a year after passing the decree, if it is not complied with, that is, the spouse who has abandoned the other does not return to the matrimonial home, the court can pass a decree of divorce in favour of the aggrieved party (who has filed in the first place for restitution of conjugal rights). An aggrieved wife is also entitled to claim maintenance from her husband. This provision was challenged (not surprisingly, as it is a grossly parochial one) for its constitutional validity in the courts, unfortunately with little success as the view upheld wa that constitutional law has no place in family laws.[17]

Irretrievable breakdown of marriage

The irretrievable breakdown of marriage is not a ground tha features under the available grounds for divorce under Hindu law, but it is a concept that courts today are beginning to recognize as valid, following the 2006 Supreme Court ruling which called for irretrievable breakdown of marriage to be ground for divorce. Previously, a divorce was regarded as last resort option, an extreme recourse and the ground provided in Section 13 sought to find fault with the othe party. Divorcees were regarded with suspicion and looked down upon due to their single status. There is now a movemen towards the Western concept of a 'no-fault divorce' – endorsed by the large number of mutual consent petitions filed in Indi today. The amendment to the Act in 1976 partially accepted th change in thinking, reducing the time period to approach th courts to one year instead of two years after marriage.

Today, in a large number of cases, increasingly, judges ar

beginning to accept the fact of an irretrievable breakdown in the marriage. For instance, in a case[18] where two young MBA executives approached the court for a divorce by mutual consent, after only seven months of marriage, the Delhi High Court held that it was not mandatory to wait for the six-month period required before proceeding for a final decree of divorce. This is a very encouraging decision, as the court very rightly observed that when it becomes impossible to live together, and there is 'complete destruction of the essence of marriage between the parties', there should be no compulsion to unite a couple, and '... it is not a hasty decision to divorce'.

Customary divorce

Hindu law also recognizes the concept of divorce according to certain customs of particular communities. For instance, if the marriage is dissolved by the Panchayat, it is a recognized customary practice.

Divorce by mutual consent

The law recognized this form of divorce only after the amendment in 1976, which added Section 13 (B) providing for divorce by mutual consent. It applies only to those who have got married under The Hindu Marriage Act, 1955 (and The Special Marriage Act 1954.

A divorce by mutual consent is a simpler and easier way to obtain a divorce. It is a 'no-fault' divorce, where both parties have decided, mutually, that the marriage has broken down to such an extent they do not want to continue in the marriage. There should be no coercion or fraud or pressure on any of the parties to agree to mutually end the marriage.

The procedure

A petition for divorce by mutual consent has to be filed by both the parties, jointly, saying that they have lived apart for at least a year and they have been unable to live together due to unavoidable circumstances, that there is a complete breakdown of the marriage and that they have voluntarily agreed to dissolve their marriage. This is the 'first motion'. The law provides that six months after this date, the parties have to approach the court again, with a 'second motion'. This time period is provided traditionally for any reconciliation between the couple. Once the second motion is filed the court, after asking any questions it deems fit, passes a decree of divorce. As mentioned earlier, the provision for filing the second motion after six months has been held to be directory rather than mandatory. Therefore, this waiting period has been shortened and it is possible to obtain a divorce very quickly under this option, if all the other requirements are adhered to.

There have been instances where one spouse has withdrawn his/her consent at some point in the case. There are different views expressed by the courts in such a situation; however, judges are often inclined to accept the view that consent once given cannot be withdrawn, and that a dead marriage cannot be revived. As I experienced, judges today also actively encourage a couple to settle the matter out of court, quickly and cleanly, that is, by way of mutual consent rather than a contested divorce. However, they cannot force a couple to settle, so often even though the judge wants to resolve the case quickly, the couple is unable to come to any mutual decision. Your lawyer, family and close friends may step in to help in such a situation.

THE PROTECTION OF WOMEN FROM DOMESTIC VIOLENCE ACT, 2005

This much awaited legislation recognizes for the first time the concept of physical, sexual, verbal, emotional and economic abuse. It provides recourse to women who suffer all of the above as well as facilitates a right to residence in a shared household, does not allow the husband to use/dispose of her property, *streedhan*, or other assets, movable and/or immovable (this includes bank accounts, jewellery, clothes, etc). The husband also cannot prohibit his wife from leaving home or force a sister to get married. The most interesting part of this legislation is that it applies to not just wives, but live-in partners and all women living in the domestic residence.

As I mentioned earlier in this book, the law books will not tell you that for a mutual consent divorce, a settlement is usually entered into by the parties, in favour of the woman (and children in the event they live with their mother, though there are rare cases where the husband receives a consideration for agreeing to a divorce). A reasonable financial package may be negotiated by either the couple themselves, their lawyers, or with the help of family and friends. The court usually asks whether the woman's interests are protected and whether she has been provided for adequately. This is probably the stage which takes the longest, as not all men believe they have a moral responsibility to provide for their ex-wives. Also, more often than not, a woman will be short-changed, owing either to the fact that she is the weaker in this respect (financially) and/or the sheer exhaustion of dealing with the complications of a divorce case breaks down any will to fight for her rights. It is thus not uncommon for women to walk away from a marriage with very little, or absolutely nothing (in terms of money and/or assets), naively believing that it is better to end the marriage quickly than worry about their security. The perception that 'you will not get much anyway' also fuels this attitude.

LEGAL AID SERVICES

The Legal Services Authority Act, 1987 makes it mandatory for the government to provide free legal aid to all women, irrespective of their means.

It is, of course, a personal decision but it may help to understand that as long as women perpetuate this attitude, change will not come about as fast as we want it. Under the law, a woman is entitled to alimony (both in the interim and permanently), as well as a residence, so giving up this right would only hurt her. Once the emotional upheaval that divorce puts you through is over, the fact remains that you need food and shelter to survive, among other things. So if you are a woman and are wondering whether it is worth the fight, all I can advise you is that the law entitles you to ask for security by way of maintenance as well as a separate residence– it's up to you to decide to choose to fight for it. If you can deal with the endless visits you will have to make to court, the tension of wondering when the judge will grant you something and how much it may be, think of the fact that you deserve a right to a dignified life; and that this is part of the struggle towards it.

On the other hand, you may have good reasons for deciding to cut off completely from your spouse; a 'sooner-it's-over-the-better' attitude, and if you are one of the few lucky ones, finances may not be such an issue for you. Either way, only you know what is best for you and what you can handle and it's a decision only you can take. After reading this book, hopefully, your choice should be an informed one.

ENDNOTES

1 *India Today*, 28 February 2005.

2 Sexual penetration is the penetration of an orifice as part of a sexual act. Defined in Wikipedia, The Free Encyclopedia.

3 Discussed later in this chapter.

4 Taken from *Frequently Asked Questions on Marriage, Divorce, Custody and Property Hindu Personal Law, A Booklet for Women*, published by the Women' Rights Initiative Lawyers Collective, New Delhi.

5 In 2006.

6 S. Hanumantha Rao *vs* S. Ramani (1999) 3 SCC 620.

7 Ramesh Chander *vs* Savitri (1995) 2 SCC 7.

8 Sarla Mudgal *vs* Union of India (1995) 3 SCC 635.

9 Sita Das *vs* Sant Ram AIR 1954 SC 606.

10 Concept of Restitution of Conjugal Rights is discussed later in this chapter.

11 *The Times of India*, 28 March 2005, 'Below 18 and married: 6.4m'.

12 Under Section 494 of the Indian Penal Code.

13 Sodomy most commonly refers to anal sex between two males, or between a male and a female.

14 Bestiality refers to sexual acts between humans and animals.

15 Reported in *The Times of India* of 26 May 2006, 'Interim maintenance default to cost husband dear: HC'.

16 Though the Supreme Court has recently pointed out that the wording of this Act is a bit shoddy – a 'shared residence' may not belong to the husband and therefore the wife would not be able to seek relief under it.

17 Saroj Rani *vs* Sudarshan AIR 1984 SC 1562.

18 Reported in *The Times of India*, 'Can't Rescue a Sunk Marriage, says HC', 26 April 2005.

4

Divorce Under Other Laws in India

The philosophy of waiting is sustained by all the oracles of the universe.

– Ralph Waldo Emerson

MUSLIM LAW

Muslim personal law regards marriage as a contractual relationship. Its purpose according to the classical law is to legalize sexual intercourse and is for the procreation of children. The marriage ceremony (or *nikah*) is a simple legal agreement. It is preceded by the recitation of verses and prayers from the holy Quran and a short marriage sermon. While divorce is a recognized concept, it is regarded as the last resort, after the couple has failed in their attempts at reconciliation. Governed by classical law rather than legislation, it provides that a marriage can be dissolved at any time, without giving any reason, by the husband only. This unilateral dissolving of a marriage is called *talaq* (divorce) and has immediate effect. It can be either verbal or in writing. When The Dissolution of Muslim Marriage Act, 1939 came into being, women were also given the right to obtain a judicial (granted by a judge in a court of law) divorce. In 1986, The Muslim Women (Protection of Rights on Divorce) Act was passed, protecting the rights of Muslim women who obtained a divorce and providing them with maintenance.

The concept of *talaq*

A Muslim husband has an absolute right to divorce his wife, orally or in writing, without giving any reason, and at any time during the marriage. The wife doesn't even have to be in his presence when he says *talaq* – she can just be informed that he has divorced her. *Talaq* may be revocable or irrevocable. There are three kinds of (oral) irrevocable *talaq*:

- A single pronouncement of *talaq*, during the time between a woman's menstruation (*tuhr*, when she is regarded as pure), followed by abstinence from sexual intercourse for the period known as *iddat* (three months following the pronouncement). The divorce becomes irrevocable and complete when this period is over.
- Three pronouncements of *talaq*, during successive periods

of a woman's *tuhr*, when no intercourse takes place. It becomes complete and irrevocable in the last *tuhr*, irrespective of the *iddat* period.

- Three pronouncements of *talaq*, in a single period of *tuhr*, understood to be irrevocable immediately after it is pronounced. This form of *talaq* is accepted only in the Hanafi School of Islamic Law (and applies to the majority of Sunni Muslims in India). It was declared invalid and ineffective in 1993, and is considered as only a single pronouncement of *talaq*, which is revocable under the law.

A Muslim man may also divorce his wife in the following ways:

- In writing: where a *talaqnama* (the divorce document) is prepared and executed in the presence of witnesses. It takes effect immediately. The wife can be informed of it after it takes effect, but within a reasonable time.
- *Khula*: this form of divorce is when the wife agrees to give a consideration to the husband for releasing her from the marriage. This could be an agreement before or during the marriage, allowing the woman to obtain a divorce from her husband under certain conditions. The divorce is considered to be pronounced by the husband.
- *Mubara'at*: this is also a divorce by agreement where both the husband and wife mutually agree on the divorce.

The triple divorce is not an approved form of divorce, though it is often used in India. This highly controversial form of divorce is not sanctioned by either the Quran or by the holy Prophet. The most famous case where the triple *talaq* was used is the Shah Bano[1] case in 1986, where an elderly woman was divorced by this method. The Supreme Court ruled in her favour when she demanded maintenance, which her ex-husband had refused to pay.

In recent years, more innovative ways of pronouncing the triple *talaq* have been reported, such as the SMS case in 2005, where a young married girl aged 24 in Moradabad was divorced via a mobile text message by her husband. While this was approved by the local *maulvis* or Muslim priests, the All-India Muslim Women Personal Law Board declared it to be completely illegal. Although there have been attempts to ban the triple *talaq* by the Indian Muslim Personal Law Board, these have not met with any success, probably due to the fact that this body is overwhelmingly composed of men.

As recently as in May 2006, the Supreme Court of India dismissed a public interest litigation that challenged the practice of polygamy and triple *talaq* and requested the court to declare these provisions illegal as they violated the right to a dignified life to Muslim women. The court put the onus on the legislature to make these reforms, saying that Parliament alone has the jurisdiction to do so, not the courts.

In June 2006, the All-India Shia Personal Law Board drafted a proposed *nikahnama* (or marriage contract), an exercise that has been carried out earlier already by the All-India Muslim Personal Law Board and the All-India Muslim Women Personal Law Board, without much success. According to a news report on 27 November 2006,[2] the *nikahnama* has been approved, and has been given legal status with immediate effect. It is quite a radical step, granting women the right to divorce their husbands on more grounds than were earlier given, including mental and physical torture, being cheated by their husbands or being barred from studying or getting a job. Focusing on the well-being of the woman, in the *nikahnama* the man has to make a declaration ensuring good behaviour. The sanctioned *nikahnama* thus appears to ensure that (Shia) women are given an equitable status in the marriage. It also gives women the right to maintenance after the divorce, until they become self-sufficient. Under the new *nikahnama* women can seek immediate *talaq*, if they have been duped and the grooms misled them about their status and earnings. It is also mandatory for the parents and guardians of the couple to be present during the marriage and details of the *mehr* to be specified in the agreement.

The Dissolution of Muslim Marriage Act, 1939

A Muslim woman is empowered to file for a divorce under The Dissolution of Muslim Marriage Act, 1939. The only criterion is that the marriage must exist when she approaches the court. She cannot take advantage of this Act if her husband has already divorced her by pronouncing *talaq*. The following are the grounds for divorce under this Act available to the wife:

- That the husband's whereabouts have not been known for a period of four years.
- That the husband has neglected the wife or failed to provide for her maintenance for at least two years (it does not need to be willful neglect).
- That the husband has been sentenced to prison for seven years and more.
- That the husband has failed to perform his marital obligation for at least three years.
- That the husband has been insane for at least two years, or has leprosy or a virulent venereal disease.
- That the husband was impotent when they got married and continues to be so.
- That the husband treats her with cruelty.
- That she was given in marriage before the age of fifteen and she has repudiated the marriage before turning eighteen, provided the marriage has not been consummated.
- Any other ground recognized as valid under Muslim law.

Cruelty is understood to include:

- When the husband is physically violent or inflicts mental anguish on his wife and does this habitually.
- If he associates with women of ill repute or leads an immoral life.

- If he forces his wife to lead an immoral life.
- If he disposes of her property or prevents her from being in control over it.
- If he obstructs her from observing her religious practices.
- If he has more than one wife and does not treat her equitably in accordance with the Quran.

Maintenance under Muslim law

The strict interpretation of maintenance prior to the Shah Bano case was that a Muslim woman had the right to be maintained during the three-month period of *iddat*. The Supreme Court held in this case that a woman had the right to be maintained even after the *iddat* period. Following this politically charged case, The Muslim Women (Protection of Rights on Divorce) Act, 1986, was passed, which was later challenged for its constitutional validity. In 2001, the Supreme Court ruled[3] that this Act was not unconstitutional at all and was in line with the spirit of the judgement in the Shah Bano case (where it was argued for the payment of *mataa* or an ongoing payment after divorce, as opposed to the *mehr*, which is a one time payment either at the time of the marriage, or deferred in the event of death or divorce). Thus, the position today is that a divorced Muslim woman is entitled to a fair and reasonable maintenance from her husband, as long she remains unmarried. What is fair and reasonable would depend on the facts and circumstances of a particular case.

However, a Muslim husband cannot claim maintenance from his wife. A Muslim woman is entitled to maintenance even when she is rich.

PARSI LAW

Marriage in the Parsi community is also a contractual relationship. The ceremony is quite an elaborate one and is complete when the priest ties two intertwined threads around the hands of the couple seven times, and asks them in Persian if they wish to marry, following which blessings are showered on them. The sanctity and commitment of marriage is very highly respected and divorce is regarded as the last resort. In the early days of legislation in this area, adultery was the only ground available for a divorce. Cruelty as a ground for divorce was available only to the wife. Parsi society demanded change in the law to suit their lifestyles and requirements, so there were many marriage and divorce acts before The Parsi Marriage and Divorce Act, 1936 (which was amended in 1988). Divorce under Parsi law can now be obtained under the following grounds in this Act, by both spouses:

- The continuous absence for seven years of either spouse.
- The wilful non-consummation of marriage, within one year of marriage.
- Unsoundness of mind. Here, this condition should have been unknown at the time of marriage and the petition should be filed within three years of the marriage.

- Pregnancy by someone other than the husband. In this event, the husband must have been ignorant of this situation at the time of marriage. He also has to file the case within two years of the marriage, and should not have had sexual intercourse with his wife after he came to know of the pregnancy.
- Adultery, bigamy, fornication, rape, or an unnatural sexual offence.
- Cruelty.
- Grievous hurt, venereal disease, being pushed into prostitution.
- Prison sentence for over seven years.
- Desertion (at least two years).
- Non-resumption of cohabitation after passing of an order for maintenance.
- Conversion to another religion.
- Non-resumption of cohabitation after passing a decree for judicial separation, or for restitution of conjugal rights (this is identical to the provision under Hindu law).

Following the amendment to the Act in 1988, divorce by mutual consent was recognized and inserted. Both the husband and wife can file a petition for divorce by mutual consent as long as:

- They have been living separately for at least a year.
- They have not been able to live together.

- They have mutually agreed that the marriage should be dissolved.
- They were married for at least one year.

Divorce petitions under this Act are filed before the Parsi Chief Matrimonial Court, presided over by a high court judge. It sits only twice a year, which makes it difficult for people waiting for a divorce. This unusual procedural format has often invited widespread criticism in the community due to the delays faced in granting divorces.

Maintenance under Parsi law

In the event either the husband or the wife does not have enough income to meet his/her needs, or enough to pay the legal costs, the court may order the other spouse to pay the costs/legal fees and an amount of money for maintenance during the time the case is pending before the court.

Sections 40 and 41 of the Act deal with permanent maintenance or alimony, payable to either the husband or wife, at the time the decree of divorce is granted. The amount may be a lump sum or payable in monthly installments and is calculated according to the:

- Husband's income/property.
- Wife's income/property.
- Conduct of the parties; and/or
- Any other circumstances.

The maintenance order may be modified or rescinded under certain conditions. Where the amount is to be paid to the wife, it can be paid to her trustee as well (a person approved by the court).

CHRISTIAN LAW

Consisting of a formal, graceful wedding ceremony held in a church, the nuptials are complete when the couple kneel before the altar and declare their intentions to each other, exchange rings and are blessed by the priest. Marriage is regarded as a sacrament and the foundation of a family. Divorce is usually frowned upon but is now not unknown in extremely difficult circumstances.

Earlier known as the Indian Divorce Act, 1869, The Divorce Act 1869 applies to those marriages where at least one of the parties to a marriage is a Christian. Both husband and wife must be living in India when filing a petition under this Act.

Previously, the Act contained highly stringent provisions under which a divorce could be obtained for a man – and made obtaining a divorce for a woman next to impossible. Christian women and women's organizations have struggled for decades for the Act to be amended and equitable provisions included. The amendment in 2001 made some revolutionary changes to the Act, and sought to remove the gender bias that was prevalent. Unfortunately, the amendment did not interfere with Section 9, which provides a referral to the high court when a question of law arises (either by the district court or one of the parties). This is a much abused section, leading to long-drawn delays.

Grounds for divorce

Section 10 of this Act contains the grounds for divorce available to both the husband and the wife. A petitioner can approach the court for a divorce under any one of these grounds, citing that his/her spouse has:

- committed adultery.
- converted to another religion.
- suffers from an unsound mind for at least two years preceding the petition.
- been suffering from leprosy for at least two years before filing the petition.
- been suffering from a communicable venereal disease for at least two years before filing the petition.
- not been heard of as alive for at least seven years.
- wilfully refused to consummate the marriage.
- failed to comply with the decree for restitution of conjugal rights for two years or more.
- deserted the petitioner/plaintiff for at least two years before filing the petition.
- treated the petitioner with cruelty so as to cause a reasonable apprehension in the mind of the petitioner that it would be harmful or injurious to live with him/her.
- the wife can also file a petition under the ground of rape, sodomy or bestiality.

Under this Act, the marriage may also be dissolved by mutual consent. Both husband and wife must approach the court together showing that:

- they have been living separately for at least two years.
- have not been able to live together.
- have mutually agreed the marriage should be dissolved.

Section 11 of the Act, interestingly, provides that if the petition has been filed on the ground of adultery, the adulterer should be made a co-respondent to the divorce petition. This means that the name of the adulterer should feature along with the name of the spouse as a respondent in the divorce petition, probably to show the court that such a person actually exists and that the petitioner is not making up this reason to file for divorce. Section 14 gives the power to pronounce a decree of divorce to the court.

Maintenance under Christian law

Sections 36 and 37 of the Act deal with alimony or maintenance – *pendente lite*, which can only be claimed by the wife, even if she has a separate income.[4] This is payable in weekly or monthly payments and then as a permanent alimony once the divorce comes through. It is similar to the provisions under Hindu law, except that the husband is not entitled to claim maintenance.

INTER-FAITH DIVORCES

The Special Marriage Act, 1954

Also commonly known as a registered marriage, this Act allows any person in India, irrespective of their religious faith, to marry under this legislation. It also allows anyone who got married under any other law (that is, even a religious marriage) in India, to register their marriage under this Act (as long as the marriage is valid). The couple getting married doesn't even need to be Indian; they can be two foreigners, an Indian and a foreigner, or two Indian citizens. When filing for a divorce under this Act, it is only necessary that the marriage is solemnized under this Act, or registered under it.

A registered marriage is usually a simple affair, solemnized in a court of law before a magistrate in the presence of witnesses. Prior to signing in the marriage register, often the couple exchange garlands.

Grounds for divorce

A divorce petition can be filed in court only a year after the marriage is registered. The grounds for divorce and their explanation are similar to the ones provided in The Hindu Marriage Act, 1955 and include:

- Adultery
- Desertion for at least two years prior to filing the petition and without reasonable cause
- Prison sentence for seven years or more
- Cruelty
- Insanity including mental/psychopathic disorder
- Venereal disease in communicable form

- Leprosy
- Presumption of death (not heard of as alive for at least seven years)
- Rape, sodomy, bestiality
- Non-resumption of cohabitation after passing of a decree for maintenance
- Non-resumption of cohabitation after passing of a decree for judicial separation or restitution of conjugal rights
- Mutual consent divorce petition presented jointly saying that the parties are unable to live together and have mutually agreed to dissolve the marriage.

The petition has to be filed in the district court in whose jurisdiction the marriage took place, either where the respondent lives, or both parties lived together during the marriage, or where the wife lives on the date of filing the petition for divorce. An appeal can now be filed within ninety days (instead of thirty days as was provided earlier).

Maintenance

If the court feels that the wife does not have enough of an income to support herself, it may order the husband to pay weekly/monthly payments and expenses for the proceedings, during the time the divorce case is pending before it. The court is empowered to modify/rescind the order of maintenance, which is available only to the wife as long as she does not remarry.

The Foreign Marriage Act, 1969

This Act relates to the marriages of Indian citizens who get married outside India. It applies to marriages where even one of the parties is an Indian citizen and where the marriage takes place in another country, but is solemnized under this Act.

All the grounds that are available for divorce under Sections 27, 27A and 28 of The Special Marriage Act, 1954, are recognized under this Act. Divorce petitions have to be filed in the district court where either the:

- respondent lives.
- husband and wife last lived together.
- where the petitioner is living at the time of filing the petition provided the respondent is living outside India.

The divorce petition also has to show that the parties were domiciled (or lived) in India at the time of filing the petition, and if the petitioner is the wife, she lived in India for at least three years before filing the petition.

Maintenance under the Code of Criminal Procedure, 1973

The Indian criminal system also provides for maintenance to a divorced woman and her children, of any faith. Section 125 of this Code is quite an elaborate provision. There is now no limit provided to the maintenance (previously it used to be Rs 500 a month) and the judge is supposed to exercise his/her discretion depending upon the facts and circumstances. However, you can file for maintenance under the personal law or the criminal law, not both.

COMPULSORY MARRIAGE REGISTRATION

The registration of marriages has very recently been made compulsory for all Indian citizens, irrespective of their religion, by the Compulsory Registration of Marriages Act, 2006. Largely a woman-friendly legislation, it would make it easier for women to prove the existence of the marriage when approaching the court in a divorce case, among other benefits. It applies to all Hindus (including Buddhist, Jains and Sikhs), Muslims and Christians.

A WORD ABOUT DOWRY LAW

Section 498(A) of the Indian Penal Code is a provision in the law that gives relief from cruelty meted out to a woman by her husband or in-laws, especially when it is dowry-related harassment. While this was enacted to protect women from horrific treatment such as the bride-burning cases we read about on a regular basis in the dailies, it is a provision that has been also much abused. It is often used to harass the husband to obtain a divorce, as criminal procedure kicks in immediately on a complaint under this section. Following a complaint under this section of the Act, the husband and/or in-laws can be immediately arrested and put into jail. It is also a non-bailable offence.

LEGAL AID

Lok Adalats are voluntary bodies for the speedy resolution of disputes.

They are monitored by the State Legal Aid and come under The Legal Services Authorities Act, 1987. They exist in every state in India and the orders passed by them are deemed to be decrees of a civil court or tribunal.

The Delhi Commission for Women (DCW), along with the Delhi Legal Services Authority, regularly holds Lok Adalats, presided over by a high court judge, to enable the speedy settlement of divorce cases, among other cases relating to marriage and family matters, including domestic violence. The Lok Adalat expedites cases by making decisions on the spot, saving time, money and unnecessary harassment. The concept of a Lok Adalat particularly benefits the lower-income strata and is useful in cases where there is no need for a formal examination of evidence. Delhi has held several such events, successfully resolving a majority of cases or transferring them to civil courts where required. Complaints are sent to the DCW.

Once you have filed your petition for divorce under the Act applicable to you, the anxiety and stress of the weeks and months during which you had to help your lawyer prepare the documents would have reduced somewhat. It will be a bit of an anti-climax, as the time for action is over and now all you have to do is wait for a satisfactory conclusion. You are of course going to have to go to the court periodically, follow up with your lawyer and deal with any harassment that may come your way from your spouse. It is certainly not an easy road to travel; there will be months and perhaps several years of waiting and many more tense and stressful moments. Under the current laws, there are no instant solutions – but if you've reached this point, then you've done what you can, and it is now more or less out of your hands.

While your divorce takes time to resolve, it is worth changing direction – concentrating on yourself, taking stock of your life and being there for your children.

ENDNOTES

1 AIR 1985 SC 945.

2 In the *Hindustan Times*, Delhi edition.

3 In Daniel Latifi *vs* Union of India (2001) 7 SCC 740.

4 Joykutty Mathew *vs* Valsamma Kuruvilla AIR 1990 Ker 262.

5

Children and Divorce

First keep the peace within yourself, then you can also bring peace to others.

– Thomas à Kempis

The primary casualties of a divorce are children. With divorce statistics growing sharply in India, the number of broken families with children is on the increase. Witness to bickering, fights and unhappy parents, children become bewildered and often frightened. Even though you may be going through a difficult, emotional period, either devastated or relieved about your decision, it is important to keep in mind that your children need you to still be their parent. Often, the build up to a decision to separate or divorce is the hardest, as it is during this time that you will be preoccupied and struggling with your thoughts and emotions. However, whatever you decide will impact your children as well, so it is equally crucial to talk to them about your decision and reassure them about questions they may have for you, such as what will happen to them, where will they live, etc. It is best to do this together (both parents) to impart a greater sense of security to them, however hard this may be. It is also important to try to leave your problems with each other aside when you talk to them. They need to know what is happening; you can be sure that the fights, hushed discussions and tension have been noticed and they will be wondering fearfully what is going on.

From experience, talking about a divorce to your children is an extremely difficult task. If they are old enough, try not to leave the discussion to the last minute, as it is a shattering experience for them. No matter when you tell them, it is always a bad time. Whatever you do, be honest and straightforward, reassure them that you love them and always will. Also tell them it is not their fault. You will need to repeat these reassurances often in the coming months. If possible, try and plan how you are (both) going to talk to your children. How they react to the news will depend on how you break it to them, and in any situation you can expect anger or tears, or both. If you can both stay calm and reassure your children that this decision will affect their lives as little as possible, you may be able to minimize the trauma they will go through. This is not as easy as it sounds – one angry and devastated parent means cooperation for this difficult task is probably non-existent. I tried to tell my ex-husband that we should sit down and talk to our children together. Not only did I face resistance, half-hearted promises that we would do it 'today', 'this afternoon', or 'tomorrow'; he didn't want to take responsibility for the task at all. We eventually ended up hurting our children, who were devastated by the news. Fortunately time heals, and love heals even more. The positive part is that with a lot of effort, you *can* work towards a better time, for you and your children.

Another important point to keep in mind is to tell them this is a final decision for both of you (or one of you as the case may be). There is no point giving them more heartache if you give them the false impression that you will be back together 'soon'.

They may have questions for you – bluntly asking why you are divorcing. The questions may come bursting out right after you tell them the news, or even after some months, after they have absorbed it. Telling the truth in a matter of fact way, without blaming the other parent, and above all, telling them it has nothing to do with them, that it is not their fault, will go a long way to ease the heartache and the wondering. The dialogue between you and your children should be an ongoing one – during and after the divorce. Give their feelings priority, talk to them, express your concern and above all give them your love. Children are pretty resilient and will bounce back if their needs are met, in every way. Suppressed problems of insecurity and fear can also be tackled if even one parent is aware of them, looks out for this fallout and handles the child with sensitivity and care.

The reality of a divorce means that children have parents who do not live together any more. In India, our extended families mean that often, children are cut off from one side of their families, for no fault of their own. It is important to ensure that they get enough time with the other parent, as well as with other family members in both families. Children can never have too many people who love them. Sadly, as I said at the beginning of this book, the number of bitter custody battles, mothers or fathers not allowing their spouses to see their child, not respecting or enforcing custody or visitation rights, or allowing very little time for visitation, attest that the world we live in is indeed not an ideal one.

There are many practical decisions to take with regard to children, for instance, who will bear the financial responsibility, which parent they will live with, how both parents will get time with them and whether you will both take major decisions together as parents. If you can handle these issues together, without strife, it is the ideal situation for the children, as it would mean a less structured arrangement for them. Ideally, they should be able to have plenty of access to either parent whenever they want to. If you can't sit down together and discuss this matter, if there is no communication or so much anger and bitterness that communicating on this issue is impossible, well, then you can expect a court battle, for custody and/or visitation rights.

Children at any age can become scared and confused if they don't know what is happening around them. If a custody battle is around the corner for all of you, the best thing to do is to sit down and explain to them what it means as simply as possible, to prepare them for the experience and help them to understand why you or your spouse are going to court for custody or visitation. They will appreciate the clarity even if they don't understand why you or your spouse needs to ask for outside help to deal with the issue. You can tell them quite truthfully that it is because neither of you sees eye to eye on who gets to have them. It may not be an easy conversation to have with your children because for the first time, it involves them in your battle with your spouse, directly. They will need a lot of reassurance that things will work out all right, either way. Ultimately, custody is to ensure the well-being of the child, physically, financially and emotionally. If they feel they are being taken care of, and that they are seeing both parents, children have a way of adjusting quite beautifully to any situation that they are presented with. Try and discuss what they can expect in the custody case – they will probably have to make a visit with you or your spouse to court, so you could explain what a court room is and what a judge does. It will help to prepare them for the visit and reduce any feelings of fear and insecurity surrounding the custody case. I told my children that I was filing for custody because I believed both parents (and our families) should be able to see their children equally, and that one parent could not dictate terms to the other – that it was just plain unfair. They understood that simple concept and were reassured that I wasn't just going to give in to being dictated to. They were also happier that they would get to see me whenever they wanted to, not when they were 'allowed' to. The point is that by explaining what custody was in the simplest terms, the fear went away and they dealt with it much more easily.

CUSTODY

The law regarding the custody of children applies to all – irrespective of religion or community. The Hindu Marriage Act, 1955 has a fairly elaborate provision under Section 26 for the custody of a child. Other laws also discuss custody though not in as much substance. A parent can also request for visitation rights of the child – which is usually granted, for instance, over the weekend (to the parent who does not have physical custody).

While the custody of a child under the age of five is given only to the mother, custody passes to the father for children over the age of five (son to the father, daughter to the mother). However, in all cases, the primary concern of the court is the welfare of the child. The court will decide accordingly, depending upon the facts and circumstances of each case. So, it is not a hard and fast rule any more. Following a Supreme Court judgement in 1999, the mother and father are both considered to be the natural guardians of a minor child. So now, the only concern is the child's welfare. If the child is old enough (over the age of six) to express his or her views and preference in the matter, his/her wishes will be taken into consideration before passing an order with regard to the child's custody, maintenance, education and other areas as the court deems fit. Thus, the factors that will be taken into consideration by the court include:

- Age: infants and children under five are usually supposed to stay with the mother.
- Sex: if the child is a girl, of any age, the mother will be preferred, although this again depends on what the child wants (if there is a dispute).
- Religion: presumed to be that of the father.
- Relationship: between the child and the proposed guardian (including nearness of kin and ties of affection); and of the proposed guardian to the child's property.
- Continuity of residence: preference will be given to the parent with whom the child is already living.
- Any other questions the court may have with regard to who would be best able to handle the financial burden of

responsibility for the child and why the other parent is considered unfit to look after the child.

REMEDIES IN EXTREME SITUATIONS

If you get custody of your child following a court order, and your spouse refuses to hand over your child, you can file a case for contempt of court. If your spouse refuses to respect the custody arrangement decided by the court, you can file in court to enforce the order. If you face a situation where you have custody and your child is taken away from you over and above the visitation period allowed, your spouse can be prosecuted for kidnapping, under the criminal law (Section 361 of the Indian Penal Code). You can also file a habeas corpus petition in the high court to immediately order your spouse to bring your child before the court. Call your lawyer the moment you feel any of the above apply to you, so that you can take immediate action.

Procedure

Your lawyer will help you to file a petition in the Guardianship and Wards Court (this is a designated court in the district courts) under the relevant clause that provides for custody and visitation in the Act that applies to you. For instance, if you are filing for divorce under the Hindu Marriage Act, 1955, you will apply for custody under Section 26 in the Act. The petition briefly mentions that you have filed for divorce under the relevant Act and that it is currently pending a decision. It will also have a short version of the facts that are contained in your divorce petition and the reasons why you are filing for custody and/or visitation of your child/children. The judge will send a notice to the other parent, asking him/her to file a reply to this petition. Once both sets of parents are represented, the judge will normally ask to meet the child/children, if they are old enough to gauge what they want. In every case, the decision of the judge depends solely on the welfare of the child. The meeting with the child is held in the chambers (office) of the judge, not in the courtroom. This is to ensure privacy and gives a feeling of greater security to the child. Questions that the judge may ask your child include:

- What is the child's name?
- Where does he/she study?
- Does he/she understand what is going on and why?
- With which parent does he/she feel comfortable?
- Does he/she get to meet both parents and how often?
- Where he/she would like to live?

While this sounds like a straightforward procedure, it can also be a tension-filled messy one. It is not unusual to hear allegations against either parent shouted in court, in front of the judge, or to see extended family milling around for support. It is also not unusual for a parent who has physical custody (that means the parent with whom the child primarily lives) to prep the child in advance and gently but forcefully suggest what he/she should say to the judge. However, it is the judge who has the final say, following what the child conveys in the privacy of his/her chambers – parents and lawyers are not allowed inside.

You can make the visit to the court easier on your child by preparing him or her for what is going to happen, in the simplest terms, including what he or she can expect in terms of what is a court, about the judge and what he/she may be asked. Allow your child to speak his/her mind – trying to manipulate what he/she should say will not work for you in the long run. I've said earlier that both parents and their families are important in the life of a child – your feelings about your spouse and his/her families are really not important here, as they are family for your child too. Both parents are important too – so while it is difficult to keep this in perspective when you may be in a state where you either hate your spouse or feel extremely bitter about the break-up of your marriage, it should not impact your children's relationships with their other parent. The more warring parents manipulate their children, the more they interfere with their healthy and balanced growth – both physical and mental. Of primary importance is their well-being, irrespective of your relationship with their other parent and/or his/her family. Unfortunately, in extremely bitter divorces, children end up with a really raw deal, often meeting the other parent only in court, during a very short, supervised visit.

The forms of custody that have emerged include:

- Sole custody – where the child lives with one parent and the financial responsibility is borne by the other. The child could also live with the parent who is bearing the financial responsibility. It all depends on the financial circumstances of the parents, and what agreement they enter into.
- Joint custody – where the child lives with one parent and visits the other according to a fixed timetable (such as weekends and half the vacation period). In such situations, legal decisions, like where the child goes to school, are most often made by the parent the child lives with. This is when the parents live in close proximity or are in the same city. For children whose parents live in different cities, only the vacation period is possible for visitation. Again, the financial responsibility and who bears what is something both parents have to sort out.
- If you are a parent who does not have physical custody but your relationship with your spouse remains cordial, try and manage a verbal arrangement where you can remain involved with your children's lives as much as is possible. This sort of informal, unstructured arrangement where the children get time with both their parents is the healthiest for them. For this to work, you need to be able to communicate with your spouse; or in the event your

children are old enough, talk to them about their schedules and how you can fit in visits with them. In today's age of instant communication, whether over e-mail, instant messaging or mobile text messages and mobile phones, staying in direct touch with your children and their routines is a lot easier than it used to be.

SIGNS OF DISTRESS

You can't always predict how children will react to the stress of a broken family. Immediate reactions would include tears and anger, which can be dealt with given time. It is the long-term reactions you have to watch out for, especially during and after divorce. Younger children react differently from their older siblings. Signs of distress to watch out for include:

- Increased bouts of crying, irritability, anxious behaviour or even fear in younger children.
- Clingy behaviour, exhibiting tantrums.
- Moody behaviour, guilt, low school marks.
- Aggression (especially older children), sleeping problems, depression, stomach troubles and regression in development.
- Insecurity, bedwetting, eating too much at mealtimes and in between meals (leading to weight gain), or a complete lack of appetite (and weight loss).
- Emotional behaviour, decreased self-esteem, anger and confusion.

- Problems in relationships, sexual activity, depression and substance abuse in older children.

Many parents, especially women, often make the mistake of confiding in their children. You need to guard against doing that – adult issues are not something you want to dump on your child. Apart from not being a healthy practice (he/she is your child, not a friend to confide in), it will confuse a child – should he or she be more loyal to you or to the other parent? Another frequent mistake parents make is bad-mouthing the other parent in front of the child. Apart from perhaps embarrassing the child, you will make him/her feel guilty, defensive, confused and upset, or a combination of all these. Remember, you're the one who has (or had) problems with the other parent – your child doesn't. Allow him/her to develop a relationship independently of your views on your spouse and his/her family – it's healthier and will make your child more confident of other relationships in his/her life. Some other things to watch out for are:

- Putting a child in the middle – if you have anything to say to your spouse, do it yourself, through a lawyer, or other adults – don't use your children as a conduit for an adult conversation.
- Constantly buying them expensive presents, handing out too much money or taking them on expensive trips or to fancy restaurants – these are guilt induced and will not 'buy' you love.

- Easing up too much on discipline. You are still a parent, so don't suddenly allow them to go wild, stay up too late or play football at midnight. Keep to their routines, study times and bedtimes. Learn to say 'no' and mean it.
- Arguing in front of your children, or blaming them for the divorce. Don't force them to choose which parent they prefer. Children understand the positives and negatives of each parent. That doesn't mean they love them any less.

Feelings of sadness and loss are normal, especially during special occasions like birthdays, or festivals. Children, especially if they are old enough to remember, will recall traditions and outings experienced as a whole family unit, and will struggle to push this memory away. Early into a post-divorce period you may encounter 'difficult' behaviour – it's just your child dealing with the sadness of past memories. The best thing you can do here is to give them space, understand what they are going through and reassure them of your love. This is easier said than done – older children will have more on their plate to deal with along with experiencing the pangs of adolescence and the turbulence of teenage years. It can be quite a tumultuous time for all of you.

Often, as a parent, you will find that you have to put aside your tiredness, your feelings and problems, to deal with your children's needs and grief. This is especially true during a divorce as it is a fragile time. To rebuild relationships, or bring them back on an even keel, even with children, you need understanding and patience. This again is of course easier said than done. Often the bitterness and heartache you may be going through will be reflected in your behaviour even towards your children. Tiredness, stress, anxiety all play a part to turn you into someone you won't often recognize yourself. Sometimes you won't be able to stop yourself from making nasty comments about your ex-spouse in front of your children, or from losing your temper due to something your child has inadvertently said or done. In these less than ideal situations, all you can do is to try and recognize them when they occur, take some time out away from your child for a few minutes or hours (even if it is in the next room) and then come back to try and talk about why it occurred to him/her. It won't always be possible for you to talk to your child – especially if he/she is very young, but you can show your son/daughter that you love him/her very much and that you are going through a difficult time. Guilt feelings about such incidents will be common but it's important not to be too hard on yourself. Don't forget that even though we aren't perfect, our children still love us. If you are dealing with a difficult teenager then it is best to let a day or two pass before bringing up the subject. In all situations though, communication with your children is the key to building and sustaining relationships, whether or not they live with you.

Some things you can do to help ease the heartache of divorce for your children and provide a stress-free secure environment including encouraging them to become independent, inside and outside the house. Give them some simple chores that they can do easily, like laying the table or helping you with your grocery shopping. It will make them feel more responsible and involved, and can be a lot of fun as well for them. Teach them to bear the pain; and that anger and sadness are both normal feelings. Help them to relax and be free from unnecessary stress. Give them space to grow into adults and be there for them every step of the way. Often this is the time siblings become closer to each other, which is always a good thing. You could also encourage them to open up or confide their feelings to a close friend or adult (such as an uncle, aunt or even grandparent who is particularly close to them), if it would help. A few other suggestions include:

- Regularly spend more time with them if you can.
- Involve yourself with their activities.
- Encourage them to talk to you.
- Show real interest in what interests them.
- Show them you love them.
- Affirm and treat their feelings with respect and gentleness.
- Be a supportive parent.
- Keep your promises to them.

- Be a reasonable parent.
- Be flexible about their weekends and vacations, as well as other holidays and festivals.

When both parents continue to have an interest in bringing up their children and try to keep to normal parenting schedules, during and after a divorce, there are bound to be areas of disagreement. Some of the areas where you will have a battle with the other parent may be:

- Financial support
- Visitation schedules
- Doctor/dental check-ups
- School meetings and events
- Discipline styles and rules such as when teenagers go out to parties, driving, etc
- Relationships with new step families
- Relationships with extended families
- Vacations and weekends.

Children can also benefit from professional counselling in the event of severe trauma or depression. So, if you feel your children need external help and support to get through this difficult time, you could opt for therapy. There are counsellors who specialize in children and you can look these up at the neurological wing of a hospital, or through a friendly network.

Ultimately, it's all about acting like an adult and being a

parent first, protecting and placing your child's needs as the first priority in your life, even though you may be going through a difficult time yourself. In the long run you will be rewarded with an improved relationship based on love and trust, and children who will be happier and healthier. Given time, most children gradually recover from this trauma and regain their equilibrium, eventually accepting the divorce.

6

Coping with Your Emotions

When old words die out on the tongue, new melodies break forth from the heart; and where the old tracks are lost, new country is revealed with its wonders.

– Rabindranath Tagore

Grief. Shock. Panic. Devastation. These are some of the emotions that will inevitably hit you when you either decide to divorce, or are told by your spouse that he/she wants a divorce. The spectrum of emotions is wide; you could experience anger, bitterness, disorientation, depression, emptiness, and mood swings interspersed with periods of grief and utter misery. Your ego may be punched in. Or, you may feel absolutely nothing – a total blank. All these are common feelings when a marriage breaks up. Incredibly, another emotion that is often felt is a deep sense of relief – at a bad marriage being over.

A broken marriage is almost like a death in the family.

When there are children involved, it is actually the death *of* the family. To grieve for what was or what might have been is normal. You had your life planned out and unpredictably, it changed in a moment (or maybe longer than that). So your 'box', where everything was placed just so, has blown wide open. To say that it is a difficult transition is a mild statement.

Picking up the pieces of your life is a continuous process of believing you can go on. In the early stages, when you are hurt and going crazy dealing with various things life throws at you, especially if you are alone, it is impossible to imagine things will straighten out. Eventually you *will* recover – it's not very easy, but it will happen; and the pain will lessen. Time, as the cliché goes, is the best healer. Once the shock wears off, and you are able to put an emotional closure to this episode in your life, you can look ahead.

Often, some people experience a harder time than others following a separation and divorce, while others may go about their normal tasks without reflecting much of a change on the surface. Either way, there is no doubt that the breakdown of a marriage and the ensuing grief will take its toll on your emotions in many ways. Divorce is a painful, gut-wrenching experience and it will be a couple of years until you feel you have regained control of your feelings and life. While time will soften the blow, feelings of pain and rage may often linger underneath the surface for years.

While circumstances largely are responsible for your outlook towards this difficult event in your life, how you handle it also depends on the support you receive, the kind of person you are and the changes that occur in your life as a result. If you are the one who decided to divorce, you will have dealt with a gamut of raw emotions before bringing the axe down on your marriage, and you may have relatively less to deal with emotionally, when the actual separation takes place, and will actually feel liberated. For others, whose spouses informed them that they were leaving the marriage and wanted a divorce, it is much harder to deal with. However you handle it, whatever emotion you may feel, it is important to remember that it is all a temporary phase. So if your emotions swing to the extreme, or if you feel nothing at all, it's all considered normal and expected. The main thing is to get on with life which, undeniably, is a lot tougher than it sounds.

EMOTIONAL PHASES

Initial heartbreak

This is the most fragile time, immediately during the separation phase. It is a period when you are at your most vulnerable. Following a separation that is headed towards divorce (especially for those who did not take the decision to divorce) you may find yourself exhibiting extreme, destructive behaviour, for instance, throwing yourself into work to the exclusion of all else, partying or shopping excessively, going into complete isolation – or, as said earlier, you may feel nothing at all. You *will* grieve, for you have witnessed the death of your marriage; to what extent depends on the individual and how you express it. Feelings of irrationality, panic, mental agony, abandonment, or anger towards your spouse are also common. So is a relationship or several, on the rebound. Jumping into another relationship when your emotions are already fragile is not a good idea at all because you are heading for more disaster when you aren't ready for it. Whatever your initial reaction may be, it will take a long time for your emotional distress to settle down, or for the feeling of numbness to recede and for you to regain some normalcy in your life.

You're halfway there

Once the reality of the separation and divorce has settled in, the initial panicky feelings may give way to a deeper feeling of misery and having been betrayed in some way. Bitter feelings towards your spouse may seep in, colouring your attitude towards the world in general and turning you into a cynical human being. Your emotions may have taken a battering and in this phase you may withdraw into yourself to lick your wounds as it were. Although you may on the surface display better control over your emotions, you will still feel shaky inside. Many, during this phase, when the reality of the separation bites, face the loss of self-esteem, confidence and even a smile. Along with emotional swings, you will have the practicalities of life to deal with, often all on your own. These may add to your feeling low and down and out in general, especially on days where things don't go so well. You can expect these first two phases to continue for a couple of years at least, until you can let go the resentment and bitterness and accept the new equation in your life.

Final analysis

Your divorce is through and there may be lingering sadness and/or a trace of bitterness at the card life dealt you. Cynicism may seep in deeper and occasional feelings of anger or resentment towards your (now) ex-spouse may continue, especially if you are having difficulties meeting your children, or enforcing custody arrangements. But, by and large, you are at a stage where acceptance has set in and you begin looking forward to a new life. In fact, statistics show that once a few years have passed, often, feelings of bitterness and anger towards your former spouse in all probability would have even receded. You may recall only a few bittersweet memories of good times if there were any, but would have probably forgotten how bad it really was. In all other ways, you should be able to close this chapter in your life for good. By now, things should have settled down somewhat, with finances, home and work all on a more or less stable plane. You can finally let go and put it behind you once and for all, and even begin to enjoy your new single status.

PHYSICAL SYMPTOMS

Often, the build up to a divorce takes years. Stress and tension become part of your everyday life; so much so that other physical symptoms are ignored, often taking their toll on your health and well-being in general. It is not unknown for even psychosomatic aches and pains or physical manifestations of stress to appear. It is during and after the divorce, however, that the tension is heightened, sometimes to extremes. You may feel at an all-time low, physically and mentally, prior to and during the separation. It may last for weeks or months. You or others around you may notice that you are not your normal self. Look out for symptoms like:

- Chronic fatigue or mental/physical exhaustion
- Unexplained aches and pains
- Sleeping problems – either too little or too much sleep
- Loss of appetite or binge eating
- Substance abuse – drugs or alcohol
- Constantly feeling low and pessimistic
- Flashes of anger and/or irritability
- Feeling nothing or complete indifference
- Anxiety, restlessness or lack of concentration
- Guilt, low self-confidence, feeling worthless
- Loneliness
- Self-criticism

- Losing interest in hobbies or other activities that you once enjoyed.

You may experience weight loss, or alternatively, a fanatic interest in fitness like going regularly to the gym to workout the stress. You may experience a lack of interest in life in general or bury yourself in one thing that interests you above all else, like your work. You may neglect basic grooming and look and feel lacklustre inside and out. Divorce can be a painful experience. *But if you have thoughts of suicide or think constantly of death, you need to get immediate professional help.* In any event, if any of the above overwhelms you to a point where you are unable to go about your daily life and work normally, you should consider counselling and therapy options.

WHAT YOU CAN DO

Along with the baggage of a broken marriage and the emotional distress you may be going through will be the overwhelming responsibilities that you may have to bear alone. Financial hardships, moving house and getting used to a new life, the stresses and strains of dealing with everyday issues like bills, cooking and home repairs will leave you drained at the end of each day. If you live in a joint family, or have gone back to your parents, you will probably be spared everyday chores and be able to spend some time pulling yourself back together. If you are alone, then it is a little more difficult as you will have to make an extra effort to remain social. If you have children, you'll be burning the candle at both ends, looking after their needs as well as yours.

If your spouse left you, all this can be very hard to get used to, even if you have family support because in the final analysis, it's all up to you: decisions, actions and responsibilities of your (and perhaps your children's) life. If you made the choice to leave your spouse, it can also be hard. You have the advantage though, of having chosen to be this way – quirky, single and determined (even if you aren't, and are a bit afraid at what life has in store for you, you *can* be sure that it is a better life you've chosen). So, even if there are more hardships than joy, at least in the beginning, it will be a life lived in dignity. It helps to try and remember that the first few years are the hardest. It could be two to five years, so don't expect things to turn around immediately. Give yourself time to rebuild your life, your finances, your feelings and perhaps a new relationship. If you look ahead with the possibility that things will get better, it is a better view than looking back at what might have been. Taking positive actions, instead of reminiscing or procrastinating, will help you to move ahead that much faster.

As I said earlier, it is important to get on with your life. Some things you can do that will help you to heal are:

- Enjoy being with your children if you have any – go for outings, activities, meals, cook with them, watch films or read together.

- Spend time with close friends – they'll help you to talk and give you another perspective on things.
- Spend time with family – no one knows you better and they will indulge and pamper you just when you need it.
- Take interest in new activities – go to the gym, learn a new language, join a yoga or art class; do things that you will enjoy and make you feel better about yourself.
- Enjoy your work; if you don't, think of changing direction to something that you do enjoy.
- Stay social.
- Look after yourself – a new haircut, toned body, new clothes – it'll make you feel like a new person.
- Start a journal, or a blog, writing down your thoughts and feelings of the past, the present and what you want your future to be. It's as good as therapy.
- Indulge yourself once in a while in something you really want.
- Get a pet – nothing like some doggy love to make you feel on top of the world.
- Renew old hobbies – reading, gardening, cooking, and music – that you simply didn't have time or the inclination for earlier.
- Experience the simple joys of a cup of freshly brewed coffee, steaming hot idlis, a fragrant oil massage, a walk in the rain, or the indulgence of a bar of dark chocolate – treat yourself. It's amazing how contented you will feel.

- Rediscover yourself – introspect to find out what you really want from life and where you are going – some people turn to spirituality to give them strength, do whatever works for you.
- Do what you really want to do – live life on *your* terms.
- And remember to smile!

BEING SINGLE AGAIN

You are going to learn a whole new way of life – as a singleton again – once you find emotional closure to your past. Some of you may have forgotten what that was; others go back to it after a brief doomed fling with matrimony. In the beginning, one may feel panic at being alone or the awkwardness of not being a couple – this is not surprising since you have trained yourself in the marriage, subconsciously, to being two people, not one. Just being alone again is a big step for some, and often the biggest hurdle in making the decision to divorce.

For those who consciously took the step, either as a joint decision, or a lone one, you may find yourself looking forward to the peace and harmony you will find being on your own. For those who examine their decision and find peace with it, being on your own can be a liberating experience. For others, it may be a nightmare.

Being single means you make your own decisions. You are also responsible for yourself (and perhaps your children if you have any and they live with you). It isn't always an easy experience but it is certainly a simpler existence.

So, it's a new life, a different one – and not necessarily a bad one at all. It will take a few years to settle down and sort yourself out – to stabilize your emotions and outlook to life. It will also take that much time for the legalities to be hopefully over and to establish your new life, home, and work and get used to dealing with the responsibilities of children, chores, etc. You may often feel a passing sense of guilt, which is normal, remembering your former spouse and life, whether or not you were at fault in the relationship. A divorce means you take a hard look at yourself, and your shortcomings, whether mentally or physically. There's always room for improvement.

Being single also means you can begin dating again, or explore a new relationship. Some may feel hesitant to get involved again, and often take a long time to find a meaningful relationship. The truth is that people often make the same mistakes they did in their past relationships and the statistics[1] of having a good relationship with a new partner after a divorce are low. This is not to say that there aren't successful second marriages or relationships – but this is not as common as one thinks. For instance, of the eight people I know who are divorced (over two generations), only two are remarried happily. And one got divorced again, after a *second* fifteen-year marriage!

The scars of your failed marriage will stay with you but a new relationship *can* do more than heal – it can bring back purpose and meaning to your life. Many even settle for companionship, which is perceived as being better than being alone for the rest of your life. I'd like to think that second time around, you settle for what you really want – not for a pale imitation.

If you begin dating again, keep in mind that you need to treat your children with tact and sensitivity during this time. If the relationship is an important one, talk to your children about it, so that they can accept this new development. For your child, this new person doesn't replace their other parent, but can be introduced as a friend and an adult he/she can trust. Acceptance is easier and faster if you don't force the relationship.

Being single in urban India doesn't raise the questions and eyebrows it used to only a few decades ago, especially if you are a woman. So you are free to revel in your single status and do almost anything you like; there really is no restriction except in the mind. Apart from a rearrangement of your priorities, your ideas, your social life and possibly your wardrobe, being single isn't very different from being a couple.

Fortunately, a divorce is not the end of your life, at any age. It makes you stop and think about a lot of things that you didn't think about earlier. And it makes you live life in the present. I said at the beginning of this book that it is a life-changing experience for many people. The point of it is lost if you don't remain true to yourself for the rest of your new life.

A dear friend once copied these lines out for me by John Gardener from an interesting book called *Fish*,[2] during a time when all my beliefs on marriage, love, and life were challenged. I've kept them close to my heart and hope they bring meaning into yours.

> Meaning is not something you stumble across,
> like the answer to a riddle or the prize in a treasure hunt.
> Meaning is something you build into your life.
> You build it out of your own past,
> out of your affections and loyalties,
> out of the experience of humankind as it is passed on to you,
> out of your own talent and understanding,
> out of the things you believe in,
> out of the things and people you love,
> out of the values for which you are willing to sacrifice something.
> The ingredients are there.
> You are the only one who can put them together
> into that pattern that will be your life.
> Let it be a life that has dignity and meaning for you.
> If it does, then the particular balance of
> success or failure is of less account. – *John Gardener*

ENDNOTES

1 In the United States, for instance, half of all second marriages end in divorce courts. See an article in http://www.bankrate.com/brm/news/sav/20000118.asp and other web sites on reports of second marriage statistics.

2 *Fish* by Steve Lundin Ph.D., Harry Paul and John Christensen.

Checklist

- If you are moving out make sure you have a place to live.
- Make sure you have all your important documents with you, photocopied and stored in a safe place.
- Put away your valuables. A woman should make a list of her jewellery and ensure she has all of it preferably in a bank locker or similar safe place.
- Make sure you have changed your postal address so that all your private and legal mail reaches you. Remember to inform your friends and family of the new address.
- Make sure you visit your bank to either close joint accounts or to open a new account in your own name. Also remember to inform them of your change in address. You will need to do this verbally and in writing. Make sure the bank

acknowledges these instructions and keep copies of the same with you.

- Before you move out or separate try and save as much money as you can because you will be faced with unforeseen expenses. It's also a good idea to mentally have a weekly or monthly budget and make a list of expenses.
- Close credit card accounts that are held jointly.
- Look around to hire a good lawyer.
- Identify and make a list of movable household items that you want to claim from your spouse. List out any property you have or own jointly and check with your lawyer how to divide it.
- Ask and educate yourself about the divorce process from your lawyer, friends and books. You should have a clear idea of what to expect.
- Consider counselling for yourself and your children, if necessary.
- Keep a close eye on your children and monitor their well being during this difficult period. Don't hesitate to ask for help if you need it from family and friends.
- Consider your options for child custody and visitation.
- A woman may decide to change her name subsequent to the divorce or even during the separation and will have to ensure she makes the change consistently where relevant. A short list here includes bank accounts, insurance papers, credit cards, passport, driving license, car registration papers, phone and

other utility bills. It's a good idea to maintain one bank account in your old name as you may receive cheques, etc in that name.

- Prepare yourself mentally for the legal process.
- Make sure you get your divorce decree when the divorce is final. Keep several copies of the same.
- Check that you have taken care of any changes in your insurance – including life, car, health and home. If your children have insurance policies check to see which parent will pay the premiums.
- Make a will or make changes to the one you have.

Useful Resources

WEB SITES

http://www.legalserviceindia.com/helpline/helpline_HOME.htm

www.indialawinfo.com

www.helplinelaw.com

http://www.helpguide.org/mental/children_divorce.htm

www.divorcemag.com

http://www.womansdivorce.com

http://www.umiacs.umd.edu/users/sawweb/sawnet/divorce/

Kim Leon and Kelly Cole: Helping Children Understand Divorce http://muextension.missouri.edu/xplor/hesguide/humanrel/gh6600.htm

BOOKS

Justice S.K. Desai and Professor R.C. Nagpal, 2004, *Kumud Desai's Indian Law of Marriage and Divorce*, Sixth Edition, Nagpur: Wadhwa and Company.

Justice S.C. Jain, 1996, *Law Relating to Marriage and Divorce*, Fourth Edition, Delhi: Universal Law Publishing Company Pvt Ltd.

Janak Raj Jai, *Universal's Handbook on Divorce Law and Procedures*, Third Edition, Delhi: Universal Law Publishing Company Pvt Ltd.

Legal Aid Services

Andaman and Nicobar State Legal Services Authority, Port Blair, Andaman and Nicobar Islands

Andhra Pradesh Legal Services Authority, High Court Building, Hyderabad 500 066

Bihar State Legal Services Authority, Buddha Marg, Opposite Patna Museum, Patna 800 001

Union Territory of Chandigarh Legal Services Authority, Additional Deluxe Building, Sector 9, Chandigarh

Dadra and Nagar Haveli State Legal Services Authority, Law Department, Secretariat at Moti Daman, Moti Daman 396 220

Delhi Legal Services Authority, Room No. 1, Patiala House, New Delhi 110 011

Goa State Legal Services Authority, High Court of Judicature at Bombay, Panaji Bench, Altinho, Panaji, Goa

Haryana State Legal Services Authority, SCO-20, Sector 7-C, Chandigarh

Himachal Pradesh State Legal Services Authority, Block No. 22. S.D.A Complex, Kasumpti, Simla 171 009

Jammu and Kashmir State Legal Services Authority, Jammu and Kashmir High Court, Jammu

Karnataka State Legal Services Authority, Technical Education Building, Palace Road, Bangalore 560 001

Kerala State Legal Services Authority, Second Floor, Housing Board Building, Thiruvananthapuram 695 001

Lakshwadeep State Legal Services Authority, District and Sessions Judge, Lakshwadeep, Kavarati Islands 682 555

Maharashtra State Legal Services Authority, High Court of Bombay, Mumbai

Madhya Pradesh State Legal Services Authority, Vindhyachal Bhawan, Second Floor, 'B' Wing, Bhopal

Orissa State Legal Services Authority, SO 11-B/1, Cantonment Road, Cuttack 753 001

Union Territory of Pondicherry Legal Services Authority, Court Complex, Pondicherry

Punjab State Legal Services Authority, SCO No. 3001, Sector 22-D, Chandigarh 160 002

Rajasthan State Legal Services Authority, High Court Building, Jaipur

Tamil Nadu State Legal Services Authority, High Court Building, Chennai

Uttar Pradesh State Legal Services Authority, Third Floor, Annexe, Jawahar Bhawan, Lucknow

Supreme Court Legal Services Committee, 109, Lawyers' Chambers, Supreme Court Compound, New Delhi 110 001

Women's Rights Initiative, Lawyers Collective, GF/FF 63/2 Masjid Road, Jangpura Extension, New Delhi 110 014; Phone: 24321102, 24316925; Email: wri@justice.com

Vanitasahayavani, Police Commissioner's Office Premises, 1 Infantry Road, Bangalore; Phone: 080-22943225.